EMPOWERED BY FIRE

DR. TIFFANY CRAYTON

Cocoon to Wings
PUBLISHING

EMPOWERED BY FIRE

Disclaimer:

This book is a work of nonfiction written from the author's personal memories, reflections, and understanding of past experiences. While every effort has been made to present these events truthfully, some names, identifying details, locations, and timelines have been changed or combined to protect the privacy of those involved.

The stories shared are told from the author's perspective as part of her healing journey and are not intended to harm, defame, or misrepresent any individual. Any resemblance to actual persons, living or deceased, is purely coincidental.

Cocoon to Wings Publishing and the author make no claims as to the completeness or accuracy of the recollections contained herein and disclaim any liability for how this content is used or interpreted. This work is offered in a spirit of truth, redemption, and encouragement to others walking their own path toward freedom and restoration.

Printed in the United States of America

ISBN: 978-1-963964-24-0 (Paperback)
ISBN: 978-1-963964-25-7 (Digital Online)

Published by Cocoon to Wings Publishing
7810 Gall Blvd., #311
Zephyrhills, FL 33541
www.CocoontoWingsBooks.com
(813) 906-WING (9464)

Scriptures marked KJV are taken from the KING JAMES VERSION (KJV): KING JAMES VERSION, public domain

Scriptures marked NIV are taken from the HOLY BIBLE, NEW INTERNATIONAL VERSION® (NIV®): Copyright ©1973, 1978, 1984, 2011 by Biblica, Inc.® Used by permission. All rights reserved worldwide.

EMPOWERED BY FIRE

CONTENTS

DEDICATION

This writing is a fulfilled promise to my Lord and Savior, Jesus Christ, for gracing me with the gift of life. A testament and proof of what God will do if you are obedient. This memoir is dedicated to every woman and man who has prayed through their pain and sometimes doubted their faith, their choices, and themselves. For fighting through every battle to gain self and purpose, to emerge with peace and the wonderment of who God truly is and how He sees you. Empowered By Fire is a form of gratitude to everyone that God placed in my healing journey who has left a loving imprint on my heart.

ACKNOWLEDGEMENTS

Kevin: Thank you for your patience and for being a part of every phase of my healing. Allowing me to be exactly who I was in every moment. Loving me. Supporting me. Supporting us. You have been everything that I needed when I didn't know what I needed. Thank you for being the father, the friend, and the confidant. Creating safety and, most importantly, nonstop laughter.

Caleb & Cameron: My sonshines. My heartbeats. You gave me a reason and purpose to fight. When I did not have the energy to fight for myself, I could fight for you. You both saved me when I did not feel I was worthy. It is by God's grace that I am here to fulfill my purpose; however, it is through your presence that gave me hope that my life was worth living. This fight back to me began with you.

Canaan & Joshua: My Grandbabies. We will never stop fighting to have a place in your life because love and the word of God ALWAYS prevail.

Rafie: Thank God for second chances. I love you, Daddy! All that you could not be for me as a child, you have unselfishly loved me as an adult and been present for your Grandkids. You are a good father and an AMAZING Grandfather, and we love you beyond the heavens!

Buttons: I love you even in your distance. I love you, even though you did not have the strength to do what you should have. I honor you. You gave me the strength to fight and break the generational curse.

Michelle: My ride-in-life sister. One of the most consistent beings in my life. We have laughed together. Cried together. Been mad together and pushed each other when we did not want to move forward. Thank you for seeing me and ALWAYS accepting me for who I am, and for seeing in me, many times, what I was unable to see beyond my pain. You helped me get here. We WIN together.

Bryan: To my brother. Who taught me unconditional love. To take the picture with those that you love, no matter what. I love you. I miss you. You will ALWAYS be my "BIG Brother Bryan."

The Haters: I appreciate you for pushing me to my purpose. I thank you for the tears, the adversity, I thank you for all the Shit you put me through. You meant for it to destroy me, yet it was used to fuel me. To fertilize and nourish my ground to be stronger and surer than ever, that God is a BIG God. God said weapons would form, BUT they would not prosper!

Dr. Cheryl: For loving me. Accepting me. Believing in me. For seeing me and holding space for me and my dreams. Reminding me that fear is not a factor because of who my Heavenly Father is. Reminding me that my "Mindset is my SUPERPOWER!"

Sister Trudy: Thank you for your fervent prayer and unconditional love. For the love shown to me daily, through a text message of faith or a hug. You always remind me to look up, no matter what.

Bishop McClary: For being a pastor that a child of God can be proud of. For all the times you were on my street, stepping on my toes because the word was penetrating my soul. Pushing me to do exactly what God has called me to do without fear. Helping me realize what I mean to God and everything that is attached to me. You are right. His promises never return void!

Mommy Blanche: Thank you for your unconditional love, fervent prayer, and holding space for me in your heart as a spiritual daughter.

Sharon: Thank you for doing the hard things with me. For being the backbone of our family and helping me do what is right, even when it hurts to be the better person. For demonstrating love, because that is how we were raised.

Crayton Family: Thank you for accepting me and the boys without hesitation, loving us as your own from the very beginning. You never forget a birthday or a holiday. Your demonstration of love towards us means more than you know.

Mo, De & Chance: We met through basketball and became family. Words cannot fully express my gratitude for what you mean to me. You embraced us and loved us as your own for so many years. You have demonstrated the true meaning of family. I love you!

PA/NY/AZ: To my cousins for supporting and encouraging me. I hope I have made you proud.

Stephanie: My Literary Doula®, who helped push this written work into being. There were so many times I wanted to quit; however, you worked with me through every trauma and pain I experienced. You helped me realize that my healing was not just for me, but it was bigger than me. Someone else's healing was attached to my obedience. This was by far one of the hardest tasks I have had to do; however, God knew giving you to me was what I needed. I am forever grateful for the gift of you and the anointing on your life.

I acknowledge every mistake I have ever made and every good thing I have done. Both have collaborated to create who I have become. What was intended to consume me empowered me.

A MOTHER'S WOUND
~ YVONNE L. SMITH

"For you created my inmost being; you knit me together in my mother's womb. I praise you because I am fearful and wonderfully made; your works are wonderful. I know that fully well." - Psalms 139:13-14 (NIV)

Yvonne L. Smith, my mother, was affectionately called "Buttons," a name given to her because my great-grandfather said she had an adorable button nose. To have a name so delicate, so kind, and so cute, I am sure my mother experienced the joy of others loving her as the first grandchild of the Johnson clan. I don't recall my mother and me ever being extremely close, like I would see other little girls with their mothers. There was always this distance between us. I am not sure what it was. I never wanted to bother her because I knew she had pains to bear. One was dealing with my father, who was cheating on her and was abusive. As a child, I did not know all the things my mother was emotionally dealing with; however, there always seemed to be a sadness covering her. I didn't know what it was, but as I got older, I would discover it.

My mother's relationship with her mother was complicated due to years of abuse by her father. A grandfather whom I never met because he died before my birth. My father was internally fighting demons as a young man returning from the Vietnam War and caring for a wife and child. I am not at all depicting parents who did not care about me. I believe they did, in their own way; however, it is challenging to be fully present for a child when you are not fully present for yourself. When you haven't done the work to heal, you leave your soul disturbed, and it isn't easy to find peace.

My mother worked hard, provided for my needs, and supported me by attending school events, providing transportation, and attending parent-teacher conferences. I remember her saying, "When you leave this house, you are a representation of us, not just yourself, so do not do anything to embarrass me." I did my best to live up to this mantra and repeated it to my children. She would arrange for me to have after-school care until she got off work. All the things one would expect a mother to do for their little girl. Still, there was that disconnect. Although I had empathy for her and wanted her to be happy, I didn't think she wanted the same for me. Perhaps she was too consumed with her childhood trauma. I did not come to that awareness as a small child. As I grew into adolescence, I was more aware of a deeper pain that not even being a mother could touch.

I would often feel smothered by my mother. She was highly selective in where I could go and whom I could spend the night with. Perhaps protection was part of her love language. Sometimes, as women, we believe that if we have someone, a child, who will love us unconditionally, all will be well with the world. Errantly, we think that it will heal the scars of being abused, in my mom's case, by a biological parent. I desired my relationship with my mom to be a fairytale. Instead, my mom's protection suffocated me.

It was the beginning of a lesson that made it clear that no one could be trusted and that most people had a hidden agenda. No one freely gives without wanting something in return.

Overnight sleepovers were a luxury if they happened. My childhood friend and I would get so excited when we wore our mothers down so cleverly that they would give in and let us stay together. Back in the day, when you stayed with your friend on Saturday mornings after eating breakfast, you did chores. My friend's chores became my chores, and my chores became hers. All chores had to be done before any fun could begin. Depending on what was going on over the weekend, we would go to the 23rd Street Roller Rink. This was a happy place for me. It is the one place I remember feeling free. I would go as fast as I could on my skates, as the wind of my movement would touch my skin until I hit that slight bump on the floor and fell. I would get up and do it again. I didn't realize then that this would be a part of many life lessons.

When I was 12 years old, I became as close to my mother as I would ever be. I had not been feeling well for some time and noticed some changes occurring in my body. I did not have the type of relationship where I could talk to my mother about genitalia or sex, or anything like that. You all may be aware of the change I'm referring to. The thing that transitions little girls into womanhood. I only knew something was happening because of the books I would read about the human body. I confided in one of her girlfriends. She coached me and gave me the courage to open up to my mother. As a young girl, I couldn't help but wonder how she could advise me on what to do, given that her home seemed just as much of a mess as ours. Their home was a mess, literally and figuratively. Their home was always dirty. This was the first home as a child where I could smell filth. Her youngest child's hair was never combed. Their clothes were always dirty. Their father had extremely bizarre behavior, which I later learned was due to an unmedicated personality disorder. It was difficult for him to maintain employment, and he was always accusing their mother of cheating on him. Even though their home had all these unclean things, I enjoyed being there because I could feel the love their mother had for them. Still, I was not aware of the intricate details of my body's changes. I so wanted to connect with my mother and find out what was wrong with me.

As I mentioned, every Sunday evening, I would typically go to the roller rink. I could escape the troubles at home there. I could truly be a kid. One Sunday, I did not go to church, and when my mother asked if I was going skating, I said no. She knew something was wrong. I was shocked that she noticed. Although she didn't seem to be paying attention to anything else, I am grateful she was attentive to me at that moment. I had been in bed all day, and when I did get out of bed, I hunched over in extreme pain. She ended up taking me to the emergency room. The first hospital we went to was bustling, so my mother took me to one that was further from our home. I was glad we did not stay at that first hospital because even as a child, I learned people who went there often ended up dying. The second hospital was where I met Dr. T. I waited for him in a cold room wearing one of those unattractive hospital gowns. You know the one you tie in the back, and your whole backside is exposed. My mother was asked to leave the room while I was alone with Dr. T. He asked me if I had a boyfriend, and I politely said no.

"You can tell me the truth. I won't tell your mother," Dr. T. said.

I was so offended. I responded, "No. I am only twelve and I don't even like boys."

He insisted again that I must have a boyfriend. With all the books I had read about the body, I knew what he was getting at. You see, in my family, we didn't talk about such things. So, I either had to learn from a friend or a book. My friends were knowledgeable, but they were also trying to figure things out. They did not know what they were talking about. I also learned from my aunt, whom I refer to as Mumtie. I could ask her anything. I looked at her as a mother. She became my mother. She became what I needed to develop into a young woman. She was so beautiful and carried herself with such grace. She reminded me of Lena Horne, the American singer, actress, dancer, and civil rights activist. Mumtie was raising four girls; she worked hard, was educated, and was my first example of a servant leader. She loved the Lord, and it showed in how she treated others. She was also very stern and required the best from you. Most importantly, she loved me, and she always welcomed me into her home. Her home was our haven when my father would hurt my mother.

While Dr. T. was drilling me, I thought about telling him about the multiple times my cousin's stepbrother would play superhero and have us pretend we were in distress. He would tell us that we needed him to save us, then, for some reason, he would lubricate his genitalia with the Avon lotion in the yellow tube. I don't recall there ever being any penetration. I do remember being inappropriately touched. I did not feel comfortable sharing this with Dr. T. He would not believe me anyway. He already seemed to think I was promiscuous. I said in a firmer tone, "I am telling the truth! I do not have a boyfriend." I had never shared this story with anyone else because of shame. The fact that I am revisiting the act, even now, makes me very uncomfortable. I had buried it deep within me, but what if, through my examination, he discovered something else? He found I was not being truthful. In my mind, I am screaming, *No, No, No, it didn't happen.* But I did not tell him anything. As I played all of this in my mind, it felt as if I was no longer in the room. I was in some distant place until Dr. T's voice started fading back in.

"Well, I have to examine you, and I will be able to tell if you are telling the truth or not," he looked at me with raised eyebrows. The statement itself implied that I was not truthful. I was a 12-year-old child getting ready to experience an examination that many women do not like to experience, even into adulthood. Instead of acknowledging my fear, discomfort, and vulnerability, Dr. T. chose to remain cold and indifferent. No empathy. I was vulnerable. Once again, alone. I asked what he meant by examining me. I knew what he meant. As an inquisitive pre-teen, I had read about the female anatomy in a book I bought at a yard sale with Mumtie. This is when I learned about an OB/GYN and decided I wanted to know more. I wanted to know what to expect when visiting a gynecologist. I learned about the pelvic exam I would be required to have for nearly the duration of my life. The doctor said, "I am going to give you a pelvic examination." He asked me to lie back on the table, a hard, cold metal table, with rough white paper that reminded me of school construction paper.

I asked for my mother, and he told me, "She is down the hall completing paperwork." He assured me I would be okay.

I lay down on the table with tears running down my face. He pushed my legs apart and forced a silver, spoon-like metal structure into my vagina. I could feel him widening the metal tool to get a better feel inside. He never explained what he was doing, nor did he treat me gently. Everything was forceful. He never once asked me if I was okay. After throwing the clear tone gloves in the trash, he washed his hands. He yanked the paper towels from the dispenser and approached the table. Again, there were no instructions about what he would do next. He opened the front of my gown and began to press on my breast in a circular motion. He matter-of-factly stated, "Seems you have a lump on your left breast. You are going to need to get this checked out."

He told me to sit up, and by this time, my mother had come back to the room. She could tell I was visibly upset. Dr. T. told her he had concluded his examination and would need to do some lab work, but that he was able to determine from his examination that I had a cyst on my right ovary and a lump on my left breast, and that he would know more after my lab results. I knew something was wrong. This is when I began to be attuned with my body. Based on my symptoms and my suffering, I knew there was something more going on than appendicitis. Dr. T. confirmed this suspicion for me. The other part of what he said scared me. I was only 12! After the lab results came back, action was planned to remove the left ovary during the removal of my appendix, and I would undergo a separate surgery to remove the cyst from my left breast.

After that ordeal, I refused to have a male doctor examine me ever again. I made a promise to God that even if I couldn't uphold any of His commandments, I would remain a virgin until I married. I still seek out female physicians and have struggled with intimacy because of encounters with male doctors. Chats about uncomfortable and inappropriate gynecological care are the conversations we are not having with our children. My parents didn't teach me to advocate for myself by asking questions like "What does that mean?" when I don't understand something, or by using descriptive words to explain my anatomy. Doing so could have created lifelong confidence in navigating my healthcare. Because adults conditioned me to accept what they would say, to be seen and not heard, I became fearful and ashamed to discuss anything associated with sex, female anatomy, or relationships. Fear can be crippling and prevent us from moving in the direction that God would have us go. The Word says God did not give us the spirit of fear, but of love and a sound mind. To truly grasp hold of this scripture is powerful, and when we do, it allows us to be unstuck in our thinking and in how we move.

Within one month, I had two surgical procedures, and the doctor scheduled an additional one. That was the summer of my sixth-grade year. I felt a closeness with my mother that I had never experienced before. We both realized the delicate nature of life. According to James 4:14, what is your life? You are a mist that appears for a little while and then vanishes. We realized we could be here today and gone tomorrow. During that season, I felt most seen by my mother. I would do anything for her, and I believed she would do anything for me.

During my seventh-grade year, in the early '80s, she brought me a puppy. A white and brown cocker spaniel. She brought her to my school with a red handkerchief around her neck. I named her "Caramel" because the brown spots on her fur reminded me of Brach's caramel candy. My mother recognized that I was experiencing many challenges by then. Girls were always bullying me. Being light-skinned, having long hair, and loving the Lord were not popular. I didn't know many black families that allowed dogs in the house, but we were one of them.

When Caramel got bigger, she had to stay in the garage. With my athletics schedule, it wasn't long before her newness wore off. During that time, I felt loved by my mom. She began to share things about her relationship with her mother, which revealed more about the dynamics of her family. She was the oldest of five children. She had three sisters and one brother. My mother was responsible for taking care of her siblings while her mother worked at a hospital. My grandfather was a factory worker. From what I heard, he was a ladies' man. Although I never met my maternal grandfather, I learned that he was tall, dark, and handsome. The family did not share much about him; it is as though there was a secret no one ever wanted others to know. One day, my mother shared with me what I had been longing to know. It would explain why I was unable to go to sleepovers, except for my one childhood friend. It also explained why I couldn't visit my favorite uncle in California, who was my deceased grandfather's brother.

She told me that the night my grandfather died in a car accident, he was with another woman. My mother revealed that he had molested her for several years, and although her mother knew, she did nothing. No one else believed her, and the abuse continued in her teens. She was afraid that he might have grown tired of her because she was older and might have turned his attention to her younger sisters.

When she met my father, she saw a way out. My mother was young, and I suppose she realized there was more in the world than she experienced in her small Pennsylvania town. She became pregnant and married my father before he went to the Vietnam War. I can't imagine being 19 years old, pregnant, preparing to care for a child, with a husband going to war. It wasn't until I became an adult woman, divorced, remarried, with two grown children, that my father began to share his dark war secrets. It explained why he was the way he was to my mother and me.

I have always had the desire to please my mother. I was willing to do whatever was needed to gain her love and approval. I did well in school. I advanced in all extracurricular activities. I did everything expected of me as a child and a young lady. It was my practical intention to please my mother. In doing so, I learned not only to please my mother, but also others, even if it meant losing myself. Perhaps it was driven by the fear that others would not accept me.

Every summer, as a child, I would stay with family members on the East Coast. Those times are some of my fondest childhood memories. My first stop would be at my maternal grandmother's home in Pennsylvania. She lived in public housing in the Black community known as the projects. Her apartment was located on Ravine Place. I made some girlfriends there that I remain connected to today. There were also a few boys I liked, but I am so glad God protected me from what could have been. When you're young, you tend to look at the outer package because that is all the enemy wants you to see. Because if you look deep into the soul, you will know that is not what God wants for you. The summer after my mother shared her molestation with me, I decided I would advocate for my mother and say to my grandmother what she was too afraid to say herself.

As a child, I was always a good listener; others would come to me for advice or to share their innermost thoughts. I always knew I would be in a helping profession, even though I didn't know what the career title was at the time. I was always advocating for someone, which often led me into precarious situations. That summer, following a strong, compelling feeling, I wrote a letter to my grandmother, attempting to reunite her with my mother. I lacked the courage to share my feelings face-to-face because I was afraid of her. I also knew she wouldn't allow me to share without interruption. We called her the "honey badger." If you have ever seen how ruthless this animal is, you would understand.

I shared the letter with my friend Sylvia first, and she asked me, "Are you sure you should give this to her?"

I told her, "Yes. I am only trying to help."

She asked me again, "You want to give this to Ms. Mayme?"

With great conviction, I exclaimed, "Yes!"

I was respectfully asking my grandmother to understand my mother's desire to have a relationship with her. To talk about the abuse that she endured. And I explained that I believed this could be the wedge that prevented them from having a relationship. Maybe it wasn't my place. Perhaps I felt that if I could help heal their relationship, I would have the mother I needed. Healing Mom's mother-wound could be the beginning of transformational healing and breaking a generational curse.

In my expression of love and desire to see us be loving towards one another, I did not expect to receive an unloving response. Whew chile! My grandmother read the letter, and she was infuriated. She called my Aunt Joyce and told her to come pick me up. Aunt Joyce was one of my favorite aunts on my paternal side of the family, who lived less than an hour away. After visiting the maternal side of the family, I would stay with my dad's extended family. I spent the entire summer staying with family I didn't see every day, something we don't do anymore.

Anyway, she told Aunt Joyce to come get my "ass." I was not a disrespectful child; I only shared what I believed to be the truth in an effort to help them mend their relationship. It only made things worse. That was never my intention. I was really hoping to help mend what someone had broken. I learned then that I could not heal what they had broken. Only God can. I did not create them, so I cannot heal them or anyone. My grandmother loved me; I don't doubt that. Being faced with suppressed family secrets can be painful. She may have been concerned about how I saw her. What she didn't realize was that I loved her no matter what. I forgave her for not covering my mother while she was trying to protect herself.

Unfortunately, we do not have conversations about abuse. We don't define what it means to be abused. We rarely discuss how to escape situations we didn't intend to get into. Shame forces us to hide so deeply that we lose our sense of self and what we believe to be true. I don't blame my grandmother for not knowing what to do. I am angry about the shield of shame that prevented the light of love from coming in. Love can cover a multitude of sins. Given what I know about the women in my life with men, you would think I would have broken the cycle of domestic violence, unhealthy parental relationships, shame, and unawareness of self. But no. I continued the cycle, making decisions out of my pain, and as a result, passed the same behavior onto my children.

One thing I did learn about my grandmother is that once you offended her, there was no coming back. She had a tough, intimidating exterior. Deep down, she desired love as we all do. Sometimes love is conditional. Perhaps after that letter, her love for me was conditional as well. Things didn't seem quite the same. Yet, she still welcomed me into her home every summer. She still loved me in the way that she could. I had hoped for a closeness between her and my mother, as well as between her and me. It simply did not happen, and maybe someday my mother could find a way to love me in a way her mother did not love her. My relationship with my grandmother was the best it could be. We never spoke of things between her and my mother again.

In 1989, I was around 20 years old when my mother decided to leave my father after 21 years of marriage. Being the only child born to my parents and growing up around adults instilled in me a sense of maturity and attention to detail that came naturally. I knew my father's schedule well and that, like me, he was a creature of habit. I calculated his drive from work to home and the time it would take him to play 18 holes of golf. When my mother decided to leave, I chose to use my resources to help her. I rented a moving truck and drove it to our family home, although it often felt like a space we simply shared. More like roommates, each of us lived separate lives, yearning for something from each other but not knowing how to communicate our fears or needs in a healthy way; we isolated ourselves. The fear my mother felt as she walked into her middle-class suburban home for the last time was evident in her movements.

"Just take what you need," I said to her as she looked around the house. "We have about four and a half to five hours until he gets home."

Throughout the entire time, we tried to be fair, but at the same time, I knew my father would be pissed when he came home. That day, I chose which side I would stand on. How could I stand with anyone but my mother? I watched how his inner torment impacted her. Although he never hit me, he showed me and taught me how a woman should NOT be treated. He was my first love. My father taught me that you never question men. If you did, there were consequences. Yes, men should work, but their money was their own, and they used it as they saw fit. Children were seen and not heard. If you needed something, your mother would get it for you. I chose my mother, and there was a price for doing so. Once we loaded up the truck, we headed to the new apartment my mother found for us. It was a new beginning that I knew would lead to us developing the relationship I had always yearned for. Maybe she could heal from all the things that she had been running from.

The enemy knows his purpose. In 1 Peter 5:8 (NIV), the Word says, "Be alert and of sober mind. Your enemy, the devil, prowls around like a roaring lion looking for someone to devour." His entire existence is to steal, kill, and destroy. When a hunter goes to hunt, they set a trap for the prey they want to catch. I am not a hunter; that is not my thing. I do have friends and family members who hunt. What I have learned from them is that the traps set are enticing. Something attractive that will get their prey's attention. Sometimes, the trap is hidden, and the prey doesn't know it has been prepared and set. It is concealed or camouflaged amongst the various distractions of our lives. You may think it is one thing, but it is something else. If you are not paying close attention, before you know it, the snare has caught you. When you think about it, a snare is designed to catch you first; if you try to escape, it will harm and potentially kill you. The intent is clear: to immobilize you. You are unable to get away. You are vulnerable, lying in wait until the one who captured you is ready to use or dispose of you in the manner they desire.

Much like the hunter, people may come into our lives and see characteristics in us that we may not see in ourselves. Like our ability to light up a room with love and compassion for others, or the admiration others may have for us. You know those people who shift energy positively when they walk into a space. There are people around us daily who do not walk in the Spirit of the Lord and loathe the light that others shine. So, they attack by saying unkind things or creating a narrative to get others to be unkind to you as well. I can only imagine what life could have been like if we were taught early about how God sees us. How do we use the power He has instilled in us? How do we walk in the confidence of the Lord? If we had been equipped with this knowledge early on, would we have made decisions that could adversely impact our lives? These are not the conversations I had with my parents. How could I? They were still trying to find themselves. When you are lost, you can't see or provide what someone else needs if you can't provide what you need for yourself. Anytime I made choices from a place of pain, I always chose poorly. Pleasing others out of pain will never be enough or gratifying for the doer. When you trust God, you become unreachable to those who try to trap you. Having faith in God vanquishes fear. These are a few words of wisdom I wish my parents had shared with me. Their wisdom could have changed the trajectory of my life and my legacy.

My mother and I became roommates. When we left our family home, we moved immediately into a one-bedroom apartment. This is all my mother could afford at the time. Neither my mother nor I had ever lived alone. While living violence-free, my mother and I were going to church constantly. I was singing more, and she was ministering. Life seemed good. I felt free, but at the same time, I was feeling the absence of my father. I often wondered what he was doing; was he upset with me, or would he ever forgive me? I did not create the situation, but I still felt bad about it. I was just a part of the way of escape for my mother.

About a year after we moved into the apartment, my mother found a house for us to rent. I was working two jobs to help my mother. I was also attending college, a student-athlete, and actively involved in our church and community ministry. Then I met him. A tall glass of water, as the elders would say. I met him through his little brother's girlfriend. She and I were remarkably close. I referred to her as my lil sister. Before she introduced me to him, she told me he had two children and a third on the way. Trust me, that is a lot for a 22-year-old to take in. I love children, but I was trying to pursue my goals and dreams. That should have been enough for me to run. I remember her saying, "he just made some bad choices, you shouldn't judge him from that. Just meet him and see if you like him." I met him. He was fine. Tall, light-skinned, and handsome. If I had looked past the exterior and examined the heart, the outcome would have been different.

We dated for a few months, and I met his family, whom I fell in love with. However, when I introduced him to my mother, she was against it. Since we had lived together for over a year, I assumed she was against it because she didn't want me to leave her. I realized later that she recognized the abuser in him. By that time, he had already given me a black eye. He was already berating me. What she discerned was accurate. She was trying to protect me; I saw it as control. I, too, had become what she was at a young age. I was not happy with my life. I was tired of being in my mother's home and believed this was the next step in life. Thinking my way out was through a man. The only difference was that I was not physically pregnant. I was pregnant with my insecurities.

My mother did not give me her blessing. Mom and I were still in church every time the doors swung open, for worship services and Bible study. My mother met a man at church (of course), whom I will call PJ. When you meet at church, one would believe it is safe. It is reassuring that there are some commonalities. It must be the Lord, right? However, I have learned that the enemy shows up at church, too. I was not at church when they first met. I saw him after they had been dating for a short time. He was well-dressed and pleasant. He seemed to be smitten by my mother, and she seemed to enjoy the attention he gave her. Being the overprotective daughter that I was, I needed to vet him because we certainly were not going to walk into another need-to-escape situation.

This was the only man my mother dated that I am aware of after leaving my father. He was attending church and becoming familiar with my mother's ministry circle, and before we all realized it, he had asked for her hand in marriage. I met with him and asked him about his intentions with my mother. In my young mind, I asked all the right questions, and he answered them in all the right ways. There was not much that gave me pause. Now our ministry family was telling my mom to pump the brakes because the relationship was moving too fast. My mother was not trying to hear it. They told her she should not marry him; they were concerned about his intentions. I found that interesting because by then I was in a marriage, being physically, emotionally, and psychologically abused; trusting my church family, who said he was my husband. How could they claim the Lord said he was my husband, yet who my mother was choosing as her husband was not. I denied what I heard the Spirit say to me and chose what my church family said. My mother chose her voice and denied what the church family said to her. She was in love, and there was no turning back.

In June of 1999, I learned of their union a week after the birth of my second son. I had been married to my ex-husband for seven years. Raising a five-year-old son and a newborn created tension. It did not take long for things to change in our relationship. Due to labor complications, I ended up on bed rest and could have used my mother's help; however, she was not available. So many heavy things were happening at the same time. My mother-in-love, who I adored, had recently passed away from cancer. I was trying to handle the grief of losing her and managing the grief of my oldest son and his father; while celebrating the precious life I had brought into the world. I was quietly hoping his gentle soul would heal the misery of my marriage. I feared her passing would eventually be the end of our tumultuous union. My mother-in-love seemed to be the only person who could reason with her son until she, too, became afraid of him. Had she still been living, she would have been there to help me care for my sons. She was so nurturing and seemed to be everything I needed from a mother.

My mother and PJ showed up weeks later. She could see the disappointment on my face, perhaps he did too, but he didn't seem to care. It did upset my mother. By the time they arrived, I was alone because my ex-husband had to return to work. I was lifting my baby boy, which was one of the restrictions imposed by my physician. Because I was not welcoming when they arrived, they left me alone, again, to care for my son. I held him and wept. I cried out to God through my postpartum depression. "How did I get here, with two sons, young, isolated, and feeling unloved? This is not how life is supposed to be. Please, Dear God, make a way out for me."

My mother and I did not speak for some time after that. My ex-husband was happy about that because it further isolated me. Eventually, my mother and I reunited, though it came with conditions. As long as I agreed with all that aligned with her husband, all was well. I was willing to play along because at least I had my mother in my life. However, during this time, I had also reunited with my father after three years. He had provided a safe space for me a few times when I attempted to leave my ex-husband. It was a tricky tightrope to manage. My mother did not care for my father, and rightfully so. But he was no longer the same man he had been when they were married. We could have a conversation about God, forgiveness, and healing. In contrast, my mother and her husband, who always spoke of God, scripture, and pushed doctrine down our throats, were unable to see past my father's transgressions.

One Thanksgiving, my father was visiting, and we were enjoying time with him, although we knew my mother and PJ would be coming later. My father barely missed their arrival.

My mother despised my father so much that they could not occupy the same space. My father was unaware of her feelings, and I didn't know how to tell him that she hated him.

My current husband, whom I had been married to for approximately three years, could see how difficult this was for me. He sat me down and said, "You must stop this. It is not your job to manage two adults. You can love both of your parents and have a relationship with them, and they will understand."

I gave myself some time to consider what my husband was saying, and I knew he was right. Managing my parents was exhausting. The next time my father inquired about my mother, I was honest with him and shared that my mother could not stand his ass! Well, that was the voice in my head, but those were not the words that came out of my mouth. When my Daddy asked, "How is your mother doing?" I said, "Daddy, she is fine. However, she does not inquire about you in the same way you do. Honestly, she doesn't like you."

I shared with him my attempts to be in their lives and not to have them in the same space. It was a breath of fresh air to have him see me and direct his attention towards my needs while emotionally soaking up the reality of him being viewed as a monster by my mother. My father had done the work of forgiving himself and moving toward continued healing and faith. My mother had been unable to move towards forgiveness, as written in the Holy Bible that both she and her husband would read and profess. During this interesting dynamic, I would withstand criticism from PJ regarding myself and how I managed my life, relationship, and my kids.

My mother and PJ were no longer in church; they became "bedside Christians." I was growing weary of respecting PJ, but I wanted to please my mother. I had learned to carry his disheartening words against me, and I was okay with carrying this baggage. I wanted my mother to be proud of me. To love me. When the hurtful words from PJ began to come towards my sons, I found my voice. My sons gave me the strength to do what I would not do for myself.

Because (at the time of this writing), it has been over 15 years since I have had an amicable relationship with my mother, I do not recall the intricate details of the day that led to the rupture of our relationship. What I do remember is talking to her on the phone and trying to muster up enough courage to say how I felt. I placed the phone on speaker, while my current husband was cooking in the kitchen, and my two sons were in the living room watching TV. I needed them to witness the conversation. I didn't want to feel alone; I wanted them to hear me standing up for them. This was important as they learned to manage their emotions around their grandparents' treatment of them. Before I realized it, I said to my mother, "I need to speak with you regarding some concerns I have." I told her, "There are several times that I have not appreciated how PJ talks to the boys." I asked her to "speak with him about the tone and words he uses when speaking to them." Whew!

The words were out, and while I took a deep breath, my mother began to yell at me. "Don't be talking about my husband like that!" Both my husband and sons turned around.

Their looks asked, "What just happened?" You would have thought I cussed my mother out. She continued her tirade, telling me I was not a good daughter. She was also upset that my youngest son didn't greet them at a game they attended. Yet she chose not to acknowledge how many times they said they were coming but did not show up or call. So, somehow, we ended up being menaces. She began to remind me of all the times PJ had done something for me and asked how I could be so disrespectful.

Because she was yelling at the top of her lungs, I told her I could tell she was upset, and I was going to hang up before she said something she would regret, and I did the same. I said, "I love you. I am hanging up now." From then until now, our relationship has been a gaping wound in my life. I have done everything possible to mend our relationship; however, to no avail. My mother cannot be the way I need her to be. She can only be the type of mother that she recognizes. Our relationship was mirroring her relationship with her mother. As much as this is true for me, I knew it did not have to be for my boys.

My oldest son could see over the years how much pain this mother's wound caused me, so he would be supportive in times when I would try to take the high road. He came with me to my mother's home when my grandmother passed away, and I offered to travel with her. She'd indicated that her rheumatoid arthritis was limiting her mobility, and I didn't think she should travel alone. While my son and I were there, PJ ridiculed him for having his ears pierced. My son was 17.

My mother decided that she would not travel with me, nor would she go to Pennsylvania. I have never understood why she would not attend her mother's funeral. Even in all we have been through, the love of God that resides in me would not prevent me from attending.

My son, wanting to ease my trauma, did what I did as a child: he reached out to my mother to help mend our relationship. While he was a freshman in college, he called her. I wish he hadn't. She did not appreciate his intentions. Sadly, she told him she did not have any grandsons and that they were dead to her. What my mother is oblivious to is that the same day, his biological father called him and essentially said the same thing. I am thankful to God that the prayers of the righteous kept my son because, emotionally, he was bankrupt.

For so long, I felt ashamed that the very woman who brought me into this world rejected me as her daughter. One of the hardest things I have had to do is grieve a mother who is still alive. What I have discovered, and have come to peace with, is that I cannot force anyone to love, accept me, see me, or to be what I desire for them to be for me in this world. Throughout my childhood and well into my adult years, I found myself drawn to women who were nurturing, women who saw me and would graciously pour into me—simply allowing me to be. All the things I was unable to receive from my mother. I have come to peace with the fact that my mother cannot give what she doesn't have. Perhaps her purpose has been fulfilled with me, and that was bringing me into the world.

REFLECTIVE QUESTIONS:

1. How do you manage one's inability to be what you need them to be for you when that person is a parent?

....

....

....

....

....

2. What is preventing you from healing the gaping wounds from your childhood?

....

....

....

....

3. What steps will you take to heal your brokenness or unhealed parts of you?

....

....

....

....

A LOVE LETTER TO DADDY

"Love and faithfulness keep a king safe; through love his throne is made secure." Proverbs 20:28 (NIV)

My paternal grandparents had six beautiful children. My father was the oldest of three boys and three girls. I can't imagine what it must have been like raising six children in a two-bedroom, one-bathroom home in segregated Oklahoma City. My father did not talk about his family upbringing much that I can remember; however, I do remember him sharing his love for golf. A little Black boy playing what most would consider a White man's sport. When sharing his interest with me, he would light up about working at the golf course near the only Black high school in the city, Frederick Douglass High School, the pride of the Eastside. He worked as a caddy to earn money for the things he needed for school and for his family. He had dreams of someday becoming a professional golfer. Yes, my father is that good. He also had dreams of serving his country as a Marine paratrooper while traveling the world and exploring photography. I am sure this is where I gained my love for beautiful images. Always being behind the lens to capture someone's smile or the beauty in nature that God created. His grandsons also share this same love for photography. Life has a way of happening. Causing distractions, some of us succumb to them and let go of what we believe is possible, instead embracing what life tells us we will.

Dear Daddy,

Daddy, you are my first love, forever. You are the one assigned to provide the example of how a man should treat a young lady. You are charged with being the provider, the protector, the one to guide the family. To be the spiritual covering of those residing in your household. These are all weighty requirements and expectations. How is a man supposed to be all these things if no one has provided them with the tools to do so? For so long, I yearned to have a father-daughter relationship with you; however, you cannot be present for me if you are still trying to fight the demons within yourself.

As a child, I did not feel you were truly what I needed you to be. I often thought you were angry that I existed. That perhaps my being robbed you of your youth. Although I realize what I mean to you now, I hope you understand this is how I felt then and what my perception of our relationship consisted of at that time. What I didn't know is that when I was conceived, the military was drafting you, a 20-year-old Negro boy, to fight in the Vietnam War. Living during a time of segregation, where being Black in America did not mean you were equal. It feels like much of what you were fighting for back then, we are still fighting now.

You were just 20 years old. I cannot conceptualize how scary it must have been for someone so young to be expected to fight for our country. That must have been immense pressure to realize you were not going off to see the world, as promised, but that you were going into combat, fighting for a country that did not respect you as a Black man. I admire you for doing it anyway, even if it was a means for you to figure out how to provide for your family, knowing that nine months later, you would not only have a wife to care for but also your first baby girl.

We never talked about what you survived in Vietnam; in some ways, I felt it through your distance, your promiscuous behavior, and your anger. The way you would become so easily agitated by a mix of a few words. Never wanting to be questioned, even if your behavior warranted an inquiry. You never wanted to talk about anything. You were so quiet and seemed to contain your emotions. I first learned from you how to keep my feelings to myself. Not to share and open up. The only time I can recall you were happy is when you were drinking or smoking. You reminded me of someone wanting to be wild and free. Maybe you were trying to find yourself, revisit your youth since you did not have an opportunity to experience singleness, realizing you have a wife who is also broken, wallowing in her trauma, and a baby girl who didn't ask to be a part of your world, but yearned for whatever you were willing to give for her to thrive. I do remember that sometimes I was a part of your world, and that was when we would go to Long John Silver's Restaurant every Friday. That was our Fish Food Friday, and sometimes we would have ice cream at Baskin-Robbins. I cherish each moment we spent together. For so many years, I wanted you to see me and treat me as what I wanted to be to you, the most precious thing in the world. I seem to have carried this desire over the years, but what girl doesn't want to feel special, to feel adored by their father? When this doesn't occur, we look to fill this void with another male. It is not just a fantasy that you see on television; it is something that little boys and girls desire: to be wanted by their parents.

We all want to be loved by and connected to someone. It is a part of human nature. I tried in so many ways to connect with you, and then I discovered something that you loved. Something that appeared to be your prized possession. I watched how your face lit up when you saw it. It gave you joy. Your first sports car was a green Nissan 280Z. You loved that car. I thought it was the most important thing in the world to you. The way you valued your car is sadly the way I wanted you to value me. I couldn't understand why you could not show me a fraction of the admiration you had for your car. Since you loved that car so much, I thought if I washed it for you, I might get a little of that attention. This beautiful little sports car was parked in the driveway, so on one cool Spring afternoon, I decided I would wash it for you. Things were going great. I rinsed it off with the water hose, then applied dishwashing soap that I had mixed with water in a bucket. After I washed it, I rinsed off your prized possession again. I tried to clean it just like you, but with my excitement to make you proud, I forgot to apply the infamous Turtle Wax. *Should I apply it after drying the car or while it is still wet?* I did it while it was wet.

Yikes! Wrong decision. Although your car was green, it looked white after I did that. I had made a huge mistake. You came outside and saw a white car, and you were livid. I began to cry while you yelled at my mother for not supervising me properly. I ran into the house and hid in my room until Mom burst in, furious. She held a long, burgundy leather belt in her hand, adorned with a gold buckle. She said, "I'm going to beat your ass for touching that car without permission." My actions had caused you to lash out at her. I have to say, you never would have physically harmed me, but Mom got the brunt of your wrath. I tried to explain that I was trying to do something nice for my dad, but I could not remember when to apply the wax. She did not care. I ran under my bed, and she kept yelling, "Stop running and hiding from me. You are going to take this whooping."

She pulled me from under the bed and kept striking me on my bottom with the belt. I was crying and trying to block the belt with my hand so that it would not hit me. She kept yelling at me to stop crying before she gave me something to cry about, as if the pain from the belt was not something for me to cry about. I was so excited to do something for you. You did not speak to me for quite some time. I never touched your car again. I wanted you to dote on me like you would your car. I wanted to be your special little girl. That was not at all possible then, because you did not have the capacity to love outside of yourself. As I healed over the years, I began to understand that you gave me what you were capable of providing me at the time.

For many years, I tried not to be in the way. To be a good kid and please both of you. Being a pleaser provided me with some safety as a child. As I began to mature, my perspective on you, Mom, and various things started to shift. I noticed that Mom worried about money, as if she were all alone. I have had a strained relationship with money for this reason. I feel that I have to be the one to provide for my every need. Not being dependent upon my spouse, but only on myself. Over the years, I have learned not to have a poverty mentality, reminding myself that I am not alone in marriage, and to put my faith and trust in God to help diminish the ties meant to bind my soul. I understand why she would feel this way. While you were physically present, you had distanced yourself from us in every other sense years prior.

We have never talked about the day Mom walked away from the marriage. I cannot imagine what that must have felt like for you. When my mother decided to leave you, I made all the arrangements. I spent a lot of time being quiet, observing how one moves, and listening to what they say. You were a creature of habit. I knew your schedule like my own. These things proved valuable when we left home while you were away playing golf. If I could have seen your face when you arrived at your beautiful home only to see you no longer had a bed to sleep in or a washer and dryer. I did not realize that providing support for us to leave would cause me to lose you. But how can you lose someone you never truly had? Years went by, and I later learned that you had to get another job to maintain the financial responsibilities that once were my mother's, as well as maintain your way of living. Although we didn't stay in touch, I would try to reconnect when I had the nerve, or when someone, like a friend or family member, shared something about you. I even went to your part-time job once. I showed up unannounced and asked one of the employees if they would get Mr. B for me. I told him I was a secret admirer.

After a few minutes, I could see you walking down the hall towards me. When you opened the door, I said, "Hi, Daddy!" You looked at me, put your head down, and asked what I wanted. I poured my heart out. I shared how much I loved you and apologized for what happened. I asked if you could find it in your heart to forgive me. I got on my knees and begged you to have a relationship with me. You were still very hurt. You said you had to get back to work. You opened the door, walked down the long, lit hallway, and never turned back. After I stood up and cried a bit, I grew angry. I told myself *if he didn't need or want me, I didn't need or want him either.* I had done all I could do. I felt you remained extremely upset about our departure for many years, and I am sure you blamed me for it. I began to seek in premarital relationships what I did not receive from you. Yes, this psychology major did precisely what behavioral experts advise against.

With all my infinite wisdom, I still chose a man like you. The hurt parts of me selected a man who demonstrated the wounded, unhealed parts of my father. I never would have imagined choosing someone who wouldn't hold me in high regard. Someone who loved me for me and would worship the ground I walk on. This is a fairytale. What we dream of is having someone who loves us so much that we would do anything in the world for them, and they would reciprocate in the same way. When I reflect on the many forms of abuse I witnessed my mother go through, I have to say I was surprised in some ways how I ended up in a volatile relationship with my ex-husband.

Daddy, this is my perception and truth of how I viewed what our family experienced and what I have overcome. Please know that I forgave you years ago for every unloved experience because that is what serving God does. You may not have been what I needed you to be for me, but you sure as hell have been ALL the things for your grandsons! You have attended basketball games, football games, and you have traveled to cheer them on. We talk, laugh, and do hard things together. Remember when we both shared that we wanted to jump out of an airplane? That had been on my "Living Life List" for a while. So, we went to iFly and had a simulated experience. I will cherish that adventure for a lifetime. We have shared our interests and discovered we like many of the same things. We are benefiting from the healed parts of each of us. I love you. I love us. You are my daddy, and I will always love you and never punish you for what was. I love you for who you are. I am thankful to you for doing the work that you needed to do to get to a healed place so that you could be present for us.

I love it when we can talk about your truth and what you were experiencing at the time. It is striking how my perception as a child is so vastly different from what was happening in your adult world. It all makes sense to me now. Please know that I forgave you years ago for everything that I thought you were not for me, and I hope you can forgive me for the ways I demonstrated my anger towards you. We have created our own love language, and it began with how you care for and show up for your grandsons. We haven't lingered over the past, but we've made beautiful memories since deciding that, no matter what, we would love and support each other, because we cannot change the past. The feeling of being that special little girl you can be proud of now exists, and I have ended up where I always wanted to be: knowing that you love me and will cherish me always.

I love you, Daddy!

REFLECTION QUESTIONS:

1. How would you describe your relationship with your father?

....

....

....

....

....

2. Are there areas within your relationship with your father that you desire to address? If so, what are they?

....

....

....

....

....

3. What is your fondest memory of you and your father?

....

....

....

....

....

THE NARC

*"Their tongue is a deadly arrow; it speaks deceitfully.
With their mouths, they all speak cordially to their
neighbors, but in their hearts, they set traps for them."
Jeremiah 9:8 (KJV)*

They wear sincerity and charm like a well-fitted suit—
something that is easily put on and just as easily
removable. If you think about it, your adversary, the enemy,
never announces their arrival. They don't hit you with unkind
words and hate. They don't call you and say, "Hey, Boo, I'm
here." They use deceit, charm, and unauthentic kindness.
When has anything that moves with the intention of taking
from you announced its arrival? A thief typically comes at
night to rob you. They hide behind a mask because they do
not want to be recognizable. Someone who wants to take
from you preys on your vulnerabilities and or assumes your
kindness for weakness. They approach you when you are
not alert. They come from nowhere inconspicuously. You

may ask, "Who are they?" They are narcissists. They come in many forms. They are equal opportunity destroyers. No matter gender, race, or denomination. They are on this earth, hurting and seeking to hurt others. In their world, you are never a partner; you are a pawn. Moved only when it serves their strategy, kept in the dark about the rules, and sacrificed without hesitation, if it meant they could protect their image. Pawns don't get to see the whole board; they only see the square in front of them. By the time you realize you are a part of a game you never agreed to play, you have already lost pieces of yourself you didn't know you could lose.

As a professional clinical therapist, I have found clients with personality disorders to be one of the most challenging diagnoses to work with. Narcissistic Personality Disorder (NPD) is a mental health disorder according to the Diagnostic and Statistical Manual of Mental Disorders, Fifth Edition (American Psychiatric Association, 2013). This manual is considered the bible for mental health professionals. As a survivor of intimate partner violence from my first marriage and being reinjured through witnessing my son's toxic, diabolical relationship, I have become a Narcisstic Personality Disorder expert by lived experiences that have been personally life altering. This certainly is not a mantle that I wanted to carry. It has been a long, hard fight to be where I am today, and I am still healing old wounds to be where and who God wants me to be. But God has a sense of humor. God said He will use my pain and repurpose it to help heal and possibly prevent someone else from experiencing the same demon.

Remember we wrestle not against flesh and blood, but against principalities, against powers, against rulers of the darkness of this world, against spiritual wickedness in high places, (Ephesians 6:12, KJV).

Because I have survived, God has given me the blueprint to dismantle a narcissist. I want to share some ways to identify deceitful individuals. They are dangerous to entangle with, and female narcissists are far worse than male ones. Female narcissists with children are unrelenting. You may ask, what are some of the signs? How will I know if I am interacting with a narcissist? I am going to share with you some common signs.

Common Signs of a Narcissist - They carry a sense of entitlement, manipulative behavior, a constant need for grandiose admiration, lack empathy, and are very arrogant. They may exhibit impulsive behavior, will not accept responsibility for their behavior, and will hold grudges indefinitely. They often prioritize their needs over others, making it extremely challenging to be in a relationship with them.

In the beginning of the relationship, they will overwhelm you with excessive attention, affection, gifts, and praise to gain control over you and influence you. Much of this behavior can be flattering and romantic, and in some instances, you may feel it is a blessing. They may give the appearance of being a Christian and pray with you while they are preying on you. They will want to know about your vulnerabilities, such as estranged relationships with a parent, past hurts, flaws, or anything else they can use against you later. They will make you feel like you are the only one in the world. They will use phrases like, "We are perfect together. No one will ever love you the way I do." Or something like, "I can't believe someone like you would even talk to me." Well, actually, they can." A narcissist does not care about you. It is all about control dressed up as affection. Everything I have described is known as love bombing. These individuals are cunning. They are so calculating that I want to share with you some specific signs to look for while sharing terms so that you can recognize the subtle signs. Here are some common tactics used by narcissists. These mimic my ex-husband's tactics, and these are some additional signs you should be mindful of:

They create complete emotional dependence. This occurs when they have trained you to believe you need them for validation, stability, and identity, especially once you lose the identity you had when you entered the relationship. You are hooked on the very person who is hurting you.

They disarm their target's boundaries; isolate them from those who can identify their tactics, including parents, friends, or extended family. However, you are permitted to be around their family and the few friends they may have.

They will gain immediate trust and learn intimate feelings and experiences from their prey. You may feel they are interested in learning about those who hurt you in hopes of their supporting you, but it is to be used later to hurt you.

They will establish complete control of all aspects of the target's life. They will make you feel comfortable enough to entrust them with things that you once handled, such as finances.

Once you are emotionally invested in the relationship, the love bomber will shift their behavior to a more demeaning, controlling, and manipulative style. The behavior can be dehumanizing, withdrawal of affection to maintain dominance, and using the very vulnerabilities you shared against you. This is twisted and demented behavior. It is essential to understand the difference between genuine affection and love bombing by paying attention to the pace of the relationship, boundaries, isolation of family members, friends, and emotional consistency within the relationship. These are dangerous shifts that take place with love bombing. If you feel you are losing your sense of self and the person is constantly trying to change who you are, run. Run as far as you can from these types of people. You are enough exactly how you are.

If you find yourself so deep in the relationship and you are not sure how to get out of it, or you have children with a narcissist, and you want to be in your children's lives, you must communicate with them. Here are some action steps to begin dismantling a narcissist. You must first understand what fuels them. What do they need to continue to operate comfortably? They need what is referred to as a narcissistic supply. This supply consists of admiration, validation, or emotional reactions; these are all the things they crave from others to maintain their self-esteem and sense of identity.

Without this consistent supply, their insecurities and self-worth are magnified.

An individual with narcissistic traits or NPD typically has a fragile self-image that relies heavily on external reinforcement. In today's society, they thrive off social media to stroke their ego. They seek narcissistic supply as a way to regulate their self-worth. You may be saying, they only seek out the weak, those with low self-esteem. This is not true at all. They prey on the very individuals they want to be. Those who are liked by others and have a sense of self-worth are individuals who are welcomed in every space they enter. They seek those who love others and dedicate themselves to serving others—all the things they are not and could only dream of becoming.

There are two main types of narcissistic supply:

1. *Primary Supply* - This approach focuses on boosting their ego in direct and obvious ways, such as through praise and compliments, preferably publicly. This looks like:
   - Constant admiration and adoration
   - Fame, power, prestige
   - Being envied and/or feared

2. *Secondary Supply* - This requires the maintenance of a supportive environment or image, which can include:
   - Loyalty from partners, friends, or family
   - Financial resources or status symbols
   - Control or dominance in a relationship
   - Emotional reactions-even negative ones like fear or anger

Why is it important to know these signs? It is essential because narcissists often manipulate, exploit, or idealize others to secure their supply. When the supply is no longer providing them with what they need, and you become fatigued by their behavior and begin to establish boundaries for yourself, the narcissist may devalue or discard you; lash out (which is referred to as narcissistic rage); they will start to search for a new supplier immediately, out with the old in with the latest. Understanding how this supply works can help you recognize patterns of emotional manipulation and protect you from entering into these negative, life-altering relationships.

Now that you are aware of the characteristics of a narcissist and what fuels them, let me tell you how to dismantle a narcissist.

1. You have taken the first step because you are educating yourself on their behaviors and what fuels them. So now that you know what they are about, stop feeding their ego. By doing so, you are cutting off their narcissistic supply. They thrive on attention, whether it is positive or negative.

2. Take away their fuel!
   - Don't argue to be right or try to win. Remain calm and non-reactive.
   - Avoid excessive praise or emotional engagement. Become emotionally neutral, boring to them. When responding this way, you are no longer serving them.

3. Set & Enforce Boundaries- They often ignore limits.

- Don't expect them to respect your boundaries, but you still need to enforce consequences.

4. Detach Emotionally- Do not seek validation or empathy. They cannot provide empathy. If they do, it is disguised and designed only to benefit them.

   - You must use emotional detachment to protect yourself. As difficult as this may sound, you must become numb and not feel. In accepting this mindset, it will help you protect yourself from the emotional arsenal they have compiled to assassinate you. Don't take their behavior personally; it's about them, it has never been about YOU.

5. Disengage or No Contact

   - Practice low contact when children are involved.
   - No contact is ideal for healing if you're able to cut ties completely.

6. Don't try to Expose or Change Them:

If you try to call them out or expose them, it often backfires. They will become:

   - Defensive or enraged (narcissistic rage)
   - Manipulative or retaliatory
   - More covert in their tactics

Your best strategy is calmness; this is your quiet strength, not open war.

7. Heal Thyself

   - Rebuild your self-worth
   - Get therapy or join a support group

- Surround yourself with others who are emotionally healthy and can pour into YOU.
- Keep in mind. You do not dismantle a narcissist to destroy them. You take this action to begin your healing journey and to reclaim the power of self.
- They lose control when:
- You stop needing them
- You stop reacting to them
- You stop believing their version of reality

Although the enemy may come like a thief in the night, to kill, steal, and destroy. The Word also tells us that no weapon formed against us shall prosper, and every tongue that shall rise against you in judgment shall be condemned (Isaiah 54:17). Fully surrendering to God and trusting Him to recover everything the enemy has stolen is a promise our God will fulfill.

I share this with you not because I have it all figured out, but because I know it will work. Continue to trust God in everything you do. Serve your soul with the word of God so that when He speaks, you will know His voice. If you do not recognize His voice, you will listen to anything and anyone.

_____ISMS

"The stone the builder rejected has become the cornerstone." Mark 12:10 (NIV)

I want to introduce you to my ism. Perhaps it will be something you can relate to as you are working through some of the challenges you may have experienced in your life. The blank is for the name of a person who periodically shows up in your being, not in physical form, but through a thought or an action. It causes you to respond in a way that you did in your past. It is typically not a pleasant arrival; it serves as a reminder of a fear, an uncomfortable reaction, or simply an adaptation to cope with something you would rather not recall. For my expressed past pain, I will refer to my ism as Chuckism. This is how I refer to any behavior from my past marital relationship that causes me to shrink in environments or causes me to shift in my confidence based on past messaging.

Part of the strength in recognizing this behavior is leaning into the discomfort of it to forge a way for growth. It was their actions that my body and mind remember. There were a few occasions when I had to face the individual, and while I recalled the fear, I was able to set it aside to advocate for my sons. Isn't it something? You may not have the courage to advocate for yourself, but you find the strength to do it for your children. It was my sons who gave me the courage to leave an abusive, disrespectful, and troubled human being because I did not want them to normalize the mistreatment they witnessed.

It is the fear that shows up because you have been hit, spat on, and ridiculed so severely that you do not feel that you are worthy of love. Isms make you feel small in a room of others. You shrink yourself because you don't believe that you have a right to be in the room, let alone have a seat at the table, because someone has told you for years that you will never be what God says you will become. The parts of you that are the residue of your pain are part of your isms. According to the Webster Dictionary, an ism is "a distinctive belief, cause, or theory. An oppressive and especially discriminatory attitude or belief." For this text, I will focus on the word's distinctive belief and oppressive nature.

To believe something, you have to accept it as accurate. If you hear it enough times, regardless of the version or presentation of this anomaly, you will eventually convince yourself that it is true. Just as you clothe yourself with your finest garments, you will clothe your soul with all the things that someone has said about you. This is more likely to occur when you lack a clear sense of self. When you do not know who you are and who you are connected to spiritually, you are subject to assuming the role that someone else says you are. There is this essential belief that it is true, much like faith. Faith comes by hearing and hearing the word of God. If you hear something enough, good or bad, you will believe it. Think about areas of your life where someone has said something about you, "Girl, you are so timid, you need to be more assertive. Why are you so quiet?" Their condescending tone conveys that there is something wrong with you. You start replaying the words shared about you, and you decide to take on the words and characteristics, finding ways to become something you are not. When you begin to be who you were not intended to be to satisfy a narrative, you lose your sense of self.

Isms show up in our daily lives. I am an African American woman living in the United States. I was raised with the idea that, being born into this world, I already had two strikes against me. One was being Black, and the other was being female. It was ingrained in my mind that I always had to work harder than my White counterparts if I wanted to experience any form of success in this life. I always had to be more than two steps ahead to establish my worth. For the majority of my life, I have walked, skipped, and run with this narrative. Always striving to prove that I could accomplish anything presented to me, even if it was designed for me to fail. We (female people of color) must always prove them wrong.

Them? Those who do not look like me. This young Black woman is built for anything. I am exhausted from constantly trying to be others' definition of me when I merely want to be accepted for being me. How many of you can relate to this feeling? It is exhausting.

In our 2025 political climate, we continue to fight for equity and equality, and simple fairness and access to what others have. It is not just a matter of race; it is the difference between the haves and the have-nots: the rich and the least of them. The very essence of racism is the position of power and ensuring that those you view as a threat remain in an inferior position. We live in a society that is blanketed with oppressive and discriminatory beliefs. Because I am a psychoanalyst, I think about the somatic system. The impact our lived experiences and generational trauma have on our bodies. How our bodies respond, remember, and contain the encounters that we have personally felt and through our lineage. This is simply how our bodies respond to trauma. Yes, I said trauma. Being Black in America itself is a traumatic experience. Partnered with day-to-day living, it can take a toll on our being.

Somatic responses can be physical manifestations of trauma—for example, muscle tension, chronic pain, or trouble sleeping. When you have encounters with trauma, you have a physical and psychological response because your body and your brain are trying to process this invasion. As such, your mind is trying to provide an understanding of what is happening and in a manner for you to respond. I am sure you have heard of the fight-or-flight response. God gifted us with this so we would have the psychological response to react when we are threatened; however, our bodies were not built to be in constant fight or flight mode. This is what occurs when a person has survived trauma. According to the Institute of Neuroscience (2022), exposure to trauma can be life-changing, and researchers are learning more about how traumatic events may physically change our brains. But these changes are not happening because of physical injury; instead, our brain appears to rewire after these experiences. I provide this explanation because not all wounds inflicted are visible.

While married to my abuser, I would sometimes pray for the physical act rather than the audible, dehumanizing insults. The bruises would fade, the breaks would heal; however, the words would linger as a mundane, sad symphony in my mind. When you truly study and understand the impact of trauma, it will provide you with a better understanding of why survivors do not respond in a manner that you would deem simple or common sense. The questions you may have discussed with friends, family members, or coworkers include why she doesn't leave, why she acts so timid or like a child, and why she is so indecisive. Perhaps it is a man who is being abused. Yes, men are abused too. Men, specifically Black men, don't talk about it because aesthetically it doesn't seem possible. After all, he's bigger, taller, stronger. And then there is the criticism. "The man must be a punk!" "There's no way a woman can overpower a man." A little petite thing can be volatile with their words and with their hands. Perhaps the reason the man is not fighting back physically is that the woman is with a man who understands the betrayal that would exist from hitting a woman. What I mean by betrayal is they have witnessed their mother being brutally beaten and vowed never to do the same, no matter how disrespectful a woman was to him. They understand their strength and the unfavorable outcome of responding physically. No matter the reason, we all should know that abuse should never be acceptable from any gender.

The first "Chuckism" I recall after being divorced from my ex-husband, of eleven and a half years, occurred after I had been married to my current husband for about two years. I am sure others may have been subtle; however, this is one that truly stands out. We (my current husband and I) were standing next to each other in the kitchen. I was washing the dishes when he reached up to grab something from the cabinet, and I flinched. My body was anticipating getting struck. I wasn't afraid, as he had never done anything that would make me believe he would hit me or verbally disrespect me. We were both surprised at my response.

"Girl, what is wrong with you?" He asked in a light-hearted way. My reaction, however, was not to flee or shield myself.

Can you imagine this happening while at work or in other spaces? Your body responding to anything reminiscent of sound, smell, or someone's action? I have shrunk in various spaces due to my Chuckism. I have often heard people question why one who has survived abuse continues to move in a submissive way. What many do not understand is that you have been conditioned to be small. For years, I was told that I was nothing. That no one would want me. That I am a girl, not a woman. When you hear the exact words repeatedly, and no one is pouring life into your soul, you will eventually believe the negative words. When you have been stripped of all the things you were taught that God said you are, it is hard to imagine those assessments not being accurate. Suppose you are isolated and have no one around you to remind you of your worth. Your disposition and how you carry yourself will not be the same. The reason you see someone carrying themselves in perhaps a frightened, withdrawn, or similar way may be because they have assumed the characteristics of what someone else described them to be, instead of what they were born to be. God said, "We are fearfully and wonderfully made." I chose to believe what was being said to me and allowed it to take residence in my being. To come out of Chuckism, I had to recondition, or should I say choose to believe the very opposite of what was confiscated from me.

This has taken years. I now understand that I can walk away from the forfeit of my character, shame, guilt, fear, and condemnation. I can clothe myself in all the things that God says I am. When you understand how God sees you and what He created you to be, it is an empowering feeling. You have confidence in God, knowing that He has your back.

How do you even end up in a situation with someone who may exhibit characteristics like Chuckism? Consider specific behaviors as you are developing a relationship with someone. Here are some red flags to look out for. When my ex-husband and I were dating, I was flooded with kindness and attention, which seems like a wonderful thing, right? I would agree. This is part of the reason you are in a relationship in the first place. You want to be wined and dined, treated like a queen. Being excessively showered with gifts is a sign of love bombing. Other signs include the relationship moving at a fast pace, pressure to commit quickly, and non-stop calls, texts, and attention. There is also the issue of ignoring boundaries. Once you're committed to each other, the affection fades. Although it may feel like you are being swept off your feet in a whirlwind romance, these are red flags. If you have a gut feeling that something is off, be sure to acknowledge and pay attention to it.

He checked all the boxes on my list. He was going to Bible study, and my spiritual mentors/family approved him. They told me that God said he was the one. He presented with great charm in front of others; appearance was significant to him; however, behind closed doors, he was a monster. Although I respected the approval of my spiritual family, I questioned whether they heard from God, because He whispered the opposite to me. When you lack confidence in yourself because you are comparing yourself to others, you may trust what someone older, wiser, and more spiritual than you is saying is true. Remember, we make decisions from our pain if we have not done the work to heal. If we have not acknowledged the pain, we are out here making decisions based on what is familiar.

Once you are love-bombed and they have you committed to them, you will find yourself engaged in a dysfunctional relationship. You will begin to experience trauma bonding. This is a cycle of manipulation, control, and dependency that leaves you trapped. You will realize the relationship is toxic; however, you will be perplexed about how to escape the relationship. 1) The abuser will gain your trust and encourage you to share your innermost thoughts, your heart. This is emotional reliance. You believe the connection with them is real, safe, and genuine, so you share your vulnerabilities (which will be used against you). 2) Their tone shifts. They will criticize you, causing you to have a mindset of self-doubt. They are the queen and king of gaslighting and will manipulate you into questioning your worth and your actions. You will strive to do everything possible to win their approval. But nothing will ever be good enough. You will always fall short when it comes to them. It is like trying to reason with a two-year-old. 3) If this isn't enough, they use emotional manipulation, which confuses. We know that God is not the author of confusion.

They oscillate between affection and cruelty, which confuses you and deepens your dependency on them for validation. Our brains are not designed to function this way, and again, the highs and lows of their demonic behavior create a chemical addiction in the brain, which makes it that much harder to leave. 4) Once they have gained complete control, the bond feels indestructible.

You begin to normalize the behavior. You start to feel as though there is no way out, due to fear, guilt, shame, or a small part of you hopes that they will change. You begin to feel as though there is no way out as the relationship continues to harm you. I know this to be true as a clinician, as well as a survivor and a witness to it by my son's ex-wife. The crazy part is that all this will be happening, however, in front of others, they will portray a disposition of a perfect relationship. Others will believe you have a fairytale, reality TV life. Others think they're an unflawed human being. When you gain the courage to leave because you feel like you are going crazy, they will villainize you to others and have their allies believe you are the aggressor. They are skilled at calculating and manipulating others into believing their narrative. It is sadistic behavior to the extent that they show no remorse and refuse to apologize for their actions. They expect you to take ownership of the dismantling of the relationship and will try to reinjure you every chance they get.

I am not trying to evoke fear, but rather to raise your awareness of how someone's behavior can create isms for you. To learn more about their intentions, to begin to trust yourself, and, most importantly, to discern and listen to the still voice inside of you.

REFLECTION QUESTIONS:

1. Before entering into a covenant relationship, have you prayed about the person with whom you are considering a relationship?

....

....

....

2. What does the Bible say about romantic relationships?

....

....

....

....

3. What have you permitted to enter your soul? Does it align with the word of God?

....

....

....

....

4. What are the isms in your life?

....

....

....

....

....

....

....

....

5. Who is in your support system?

....

....

....

....

....

....

....

....

H.E.R
HURTFUL. EXPOSED. RAGE.

If I had just expressed to him how much I did not agree with this relationship, would we be where we are now? If I had been more assertive and inserted myself, would we be here? When my husband said, "If she is spitting and hitting on you now, it is just going to get worse," should I have stood united with my husband? When my youngest adult son stated, "I peeped the energy before wanting to make a connection. So, I did not get with her or her family like that." Should I have heeded his pause?

As I write these questions, my brain is screaming 'YES!' Girl, what were you thinking? Why didn't you do more? I continue to play the questions in my mind while I live with the residue of my son surviving the wrath of a narcissist. And the effects of H.E.R. on our family. It is true; when you say 'I do' to your spouse, you are also saying 'I do' to the family. Everyone is impacted for better or for worse. The woman my son married had the same toxicity as my ex-husband.

Reliving that trauma through him is something I would not want anyone to have to endure.

According to the Centers for Disease Control and Prevention (CDC, 2024), domestic violence is physical violence, sexual violence, stalking, and psychological aggression (including coercive acts) by a current or former intimate partner. According to the CDC's National Intimate Partner and Sexual Violence Survey (NISVS), 1 in 4 women and 1 in 7 men will experience physical violence by their intimate partner at some point during their lifetime. About 1 in 3 women and nearly 1 in 6 men experience some form of sexual violence during their lifetimes (CDC, 2024). These are statistics that I did not want either of my sons to experience. I had done all the things to prevent them from experiencing the depths of abuse I had experienced. One would never think that sharing your heart and fears would be used to hurt you even more.

What saddens me is that not only did both of my sons endure the abuse they witnessed by their biological father, but my oldest son was also reinjured, finding himself surviving a toxic, tumultuous, abusive marriage. I did not believe a woman could inflict so much physical, psychological, and emotional pain on a man until it was in living color in my world. God, we've already talked about this. Why is this happening again? I thought I had done everything to ensure my sons were good. Well, when did I become God? When did I become the ruler over their lives, believing I could control everything? Although God used me to bring them into this world, I did not create them. I have come to realize that, despite my good intentions, I am not in control of anything. The decisions my children make do not obligate me to correct them if I have given them back to God.

Intimate partner violence, sexual violence, and stalking are high, with intimate partner violence alone affecting over 10 million people each year. Things I knew as a trained trauma-informed terminal degree clinician; however, things did not become real until these hurtful deeds hit me smack dab in the face. I always taught my sons to be young men who treated women with respect. To care for a young lady like a queen. I taught them how to care for themselves domestically so they would not depend on a woman to manage what society considers "domesticated" duties. Truly to be of service to one another. To work hard and take care of their families. I would show them examples of girls and women who are not suitable to bring home due to their "loose" dispositions. I was intentional in teaching them how not to be like their biological father.

I never discussed with them the importance of recognizing the signs of engaging with a woman who could be like their father—emasculating with their tongue, doling out silent and cruel treatment when they did not get their way, or hitting or spitting on them, and gaslighting so severely that you begin to question your sensibility and reality. They were brought up not to be abusers but not taught how to recognize the abuser, nor what to do if they were abused.

We often hear of women being abused, not men. I never saw a man being abused in my family, only women. I taught from my frame of reference, but then we met H.E.R. Taking time to get to know your potential partner is vital. Being with them through various life and emotional seasons reveals how they will respond to the best and worst of you. Will they be with you when you are financially challenged and when you are emotionally bankrupt? Of course, this all makes sense; who would not consider these things when dating?

One of the most important things, aside from what has been previously described, is whether they have a relationship with Christ. Let me be clear: a relationship is different from attending church, professing love for the Lord, conducting Bible studies, or praying before meals or on special holidays. Just because a parent is an ordained minister does not automatically give them a pass to holiness. It is in how you treat others. How do you live your life when no one is watching? When you recognize that others in your family are not moving in the teachings that you profess, will you say something? Or will you stand by as a spectator, or fail to acknowledge what is happening around you? Or when asked for help, say it is not your problem. I am a firm believer in watching how one moves, not simply hearing the words coming out of their mouth. What I know to be true is that one has gained in the number of living years, but that does not mean they are mature with wisdom. H.E.R.'s parents are older than my husband and me. We expected them to have greater insight and less tolerance of nonsense. We expected them to have greater insight and less tolerance of nonsense. You often expect that if someone is older than you, they must be wiser. For me, when someone is older and they profess to know "the Word," the Bible, I expect more from them. I expect them to do the right thing according to the Bible. Although we often expect older individuals to behave in an honorable and respectful manner, this is not always the case.

Before meeting this young lady and knowing the status of their relationship, I received a three-way call from her and her sister. I was leaving work and heading home. Our son had been with them at a local club, and they mentioned he had received a call from his biological father. Our son was visibly upset, which concerned them. I shared some context to help them understand the estranged, messy relationship with his biological father. I felt an unsettling sensation in my gut about the call, as it seemed they were more concerned with appearances than with what was actually happening to him. I minimized my feelings by reading more into it than necessary. I thought what they demonstrated was some kindness. I later learned my discernment was correct; however, the details of those things are for our son to share. When you have survived intimate partner violence (IPV), you tend to second-guess most things. You do not trust your intuition because you feel it can't be trusted. You focus on all the things you didn't get right. You cannot trust any decisions you attempt to make because the one decision you made cost you so much.

When we first met H.E.R., our oldest son had invited us to have dinner at a local restaurant. I could tell she was nervous; who wouldn't be when you're meeting your boyfriend's parents for the first time? I say "boyfriend" as this is what one would assume. Our son didn't bring her around the family, so we never had the chance to get to know her. This behavior was different, but it is one of those things you notice without making a big deal out of it. I am sure that if we had the opportunity to interact with her, our immediate and extended family would have observed her behavior and would have been able to share our concerns. Still, we did not have that opportunity, and now we are feeling the aftermath.

We were having a pleasant dinner, and I was trying not to be too intrusive, but I wanted to be friendly. She was not rude but reserved. Again, this may be attributed to nervousness and uncertainty about what to expect. While sitting in the booth, the light gleamed off her skin. It was as if she were glowing. Smooth skin, big curly hair, petite. All things a young 24-year-old man would find attractive. Our son seemed proud to have her on his arm. She was gorgeous, all things aesthetically pleasing. When I think of beautiful gifts, I think about packaging. How lovely it is on the outside. The perfectly arranged bow, the bright, neatly seamed wrapping paper. The ornament that's placed on the package gives it that extra special touch. It gives the appearance that the contents inside will match the dynamic presentation of what you see on the outside, but when you open the package, the contents inside don't align with what you are seeing on the outside. You feel you have been tricked. You have been hoodwinked. I have learned a painful lesson. People will allow you to see what they want you to see. Again, pay attention to how people move. Check if what they are saying aligns with their actions. Although she was beautiful on the outside, she did not demonstrate love or empathy for others.

I inquired about where they met, and our son mentioned a party, then quickly began discussing Bible study. For some reason, when he discussed the Bible study she and her sister organized, my reservations lightened. Don't be fooled. What one needs to understand is that just because one mentions Jesus doesn't mean He resides within. The devil shows up at Bible study and churches every week. I have discovered that some use the name of Jesus as though He is an accessory that we add to our attire. As the conversation continued, our son blurted out that she is going to be his wife. My husband and I both choked on our food, and she seemed petrified. She began to bite her bottom lip and seemed a bit irritated.

To break the awkwardness, I said to our son, "It seems as though she is surprised by this announcement and a little uncomfortable." I tried to console her and make light of the uncomfortable feelings we were all experiencing.

While driving home, my husband and I talked, and he said he couldn't put his finger on it, but something didn't seem quite right. "We are just meeting this girl, and he is talking about marriage?" He thought it was too soon. We didn't even know her.

The next day, I talked to our son, and he apologized. He said she was upset with him. He was going on and on about how she does not like to be caught off guard, and although she was upset, they talked about it. He said he was just excited. She was everything he asked for. She was pretty, loved the Lord, and was educated, seeming to know what she wanted in life. Our son had been back home only a short time after playing ball overseas, had an apartment, and was trying to establish himself. I recall him mentioning his girlfriend was staying with him while she used her home as an Airbnb. Although this gave me pause, he shared with me a time when he had shared his innermost feelings, and she prayed with him. Again, my concern for what was happening was silenced. She prayed with him. What a beautiful thing to have someone pray with you. Even the enemy can present things in a way to distract you from what you need to see. The enemy comes to kill, steal, and destroy.

According to 1 Peter 5:8 (NIV), we should, "Be alert and of sober mind. Your enemy the devil prowls around like a roaring lion looking for someone to devour." Now, in hindsight, it reminds me of the story of Jezebel. (I would encourage you to read the story.) What I will say is that Jezebel is one of the first representations in the Bible of one's ability to create a space through her craftiness, cruelty, maliciousness, and revengeful behavior to destroy others for her gain. She exhibited no empathy; she was guided by her own principles and spared no pain. She is our first example of a female narcissist. Jezebel's story is one of a loose woman who carried herself in a promiscuous manner. My Lord, if I had known more about her characteristics, I could have shared this with my sons during their upbringing. My focus would not have been so much on the promiscuous behavior of some young ladies.

It had been approximately three months since we had dinner with the young couple, and our son's birthday was coming up. He is a February baby. I was trying so hard to deliver him on February 14th, but God had a different plan; he was born on February 15th. We always had to share his birthday with a basketball game. So, we would try to make it as special as we could. That year, it was for a different reason; he was not playing ball; however, he seemed consumed with making Valentine's Day memorable for her. She was expecting him to propose, and it had to be something grand. He was extremely worried that if he didn't plan something big enough, something would happen. That concerned me. Given how close we are, I didn't want to come across as overbearing and interfering with his life decisions. Recalling what I learned in my psychology classes, if I shared my reservations about this relationship, it would likely cause them to draw even closer.

As I reflect on their short courtship, I do not recall there being a time when she attempted to learn anything from us about our son. What he likes, what he was like as a child, nothing that would help her understand the manifestation of who he is as a young man. There was no intentionality in getting to know us. To be around anyone in our family. Again, a red flag. Anyone who knows me knows that I am approachable. That I am loving and lead with a servant's heart. Our son did not propose to her, and he later shared with us how upset she was that he had not done so. This is when I began to realize that appearance is important to her. It wasn't long after this incident that he proposed. Although the social media post depicted a happy, loving couple, the reality was far from it. Our son discussed the criticism of all the things that were not done correctly, from what he was wearing to how he proposed. Again, these statements are from the perspective of our son. Things seemed to be moving fast. My husband was not saying much, but his disposition demonstrated he had reservations regarding this potential union. As they continued to take steps, there seemed to be an isolation of family members. Not at all what one would view as customary when uniting families in marriage.

The soon-to-be bride was making wedding plans. Her mother and I were getting to know each other and spending time weekly to find the traditional mother-of-the-bride and mother-of-the-groom attire for the wedding. There was always this uneasiness, a feeling of a lack of authenticity when I was around H.E.R.'s mother and siblings, but I continued to go with the flow of things. I was beginning to develop feelings of timidness, fear, and a reluctance to rock the boat, and I was made to feel guilty for making decisions.

Much of what my oldest was experiencing was triggering things in me that had been lying dormant for years. I know. Why didn't I say something? Why didn't I do more? When you haven't addressed your own trauma and you have not healed from your past wounds, it is hard to help someone else, even when it is your own son. Trust me, I have replayed many things in my head over and over again. I have cried and, at times, started to believe many of the cruel things this woman has said about me as a mother. Until I gave H.E.R. and this entire situation to God, to be fully present for others, you first must be healed and present for yourself.

Our son was making financial decisions that didn't seem to be based on much thought. He decided to move from the apartment he was residing in because she did not feel safe there, so they moved to another apartment in Dallas that did not appear to be safer than where he was. Then, shortly before they married, they abruptly broke the lease on that apartment and asked for financial assistance. The fiancé's mother reached out to me and asked what I would be able to pay to help get the kids out of a dangerous environment. Against my better judgment, I spent half of what was owed. When the soon-to-be bride was looking for venues for the wedding, I was invited, not because I am the mother of the groom, but for financial reasons. The venue was gorgeous. Shortly afterwards, I was asked to pay half of that cost. Traditionally, the bride's parents assume responsibility for the wedding costs. The father of the bride had made it clear he would not be offering any financial support for a lavish wedding. The inactivity or presence of both men, fathers in the family, should have been another clue of misalignment. A date had been set, and the couple desired that venue for their wedding. I say "couple" loosely, as I was quickly learning that it was really whatever she wanted. I suppose my son was willing to do whatever she wanted to keep the peace. This is not unusual behavior when you are with an abuser. You lose your sense of self. You are not capable of making your own decisions because you have been conditioned to do whatever it takes to keep the peace. This can be a difficult concept to understand if you have never been in an intimate partner violence situation. Be careful not to reveal what you would or would not do, because once you realize your role, you may not know how to escape it.

While pushing this venue, I would later learn they were already married. I paid for half of the venue, only to be treated like the hired help on the wedding day. The date had been determined, and when we requested to change the date so our youngest son could be present, they said no. July 3, 2019, was the day. A week before their wedding, our son came to our home. He was visibly upset. He had been crying and had a deep gash on the right side of his face. The skin around his eye was a blackish-blue color as he shared his pain.

I called my husband to join us at the kitchen counter. I asked my son, "Who did this to you? Did she hit you?" His wound was a scratch that appeared to be something only a woman would do. I pulled out my phone to take a picture. He asked me not to do it. He was so embarrassed. I said, "No, I am taking this picture," not knowing that a few years later the picture would be used during their divorce proceedings.

He began to weep. He shared with us that she had spat on him and struck him several times. I am sure you have heard mothers defend their sons in the worst of times, even when their son may have done something wrong. Those who know us know this is not true. Our sons know it is not true.

If you have done something wrong, we will be the first to tell you. I know within my heart that my son has never and will never hit a woman because of the pain and anguish that he witnessed me go through.

My husband told our son, "If she is whooping, your ass now, she will continue to do so. It will only get worse. There is no way I would be with someone who would treat me this way. She spat on you, too! I cannot support this union."

When I looked at my son, I could see myself. The pain and confusion were so deep. He did love her and wanted to prove to himself that he could make things work. With a wedding a week away, he thought of all the money that had been spent. What will people think? I wish he had the courage to get out. I wish I had said and done more. Who you marry is one of the most important decisions you'll ever make in your life. Please be mindful of what you are attaching yourself to, spiritually and generationally.

Both of my sons graduated from high school with good grades and went on to become phenomenal athletes. They also graduated from college with no legal infractions and no children out of wedlock, experiencing many successes along the way. How is it possible that we are reliving a pain that has been in our family from one generation to the next? I honestly thought the generational curse had been broken. As I looked at my son, I told him not to go through with it. He began to sound like I did as a battered woman. *If I just learn how to communicate better, if I just...* He made so many excuses for her behavior. It is never okay for someone to put their hands on you or spit on you. This is one of the most dehumanizing things a person can do to you. I remember when their biological father spat on me. It was as if everything I had gone through was happening to him with her. Everything he shared about what he witnessed was being used against him by her. It is a sick, demented individual who will use your vulnerability and pain against you.

While he was weeping, he was saying, "I just don't know how to get out of it." He suggested that we all sit down as a family and discuss it. Maybe that would help. A few days later, my husband, our son, his fiancée, I, and her mother met at a restaurant that her brother managed. Her father did not show up. My husband did not appreciate his being absent. I am still unsure whether he was aware that the meeting was taking place and that his daughter had difficulties keeping her hands to herself. We were sitting there having a conversation about the inappropriate behavior that was happening in their relationship, and it didn't seem like a big deal to her and her mother. The mother suggested that they needed to improve their communication skills, and it was just the stress of getting ready for the big day. My husband and I discussed marriage being more than just the big day. Marriage is work and selflessness. The conversation was going in circles. The Holy Spirit urged me to ask one question. I asked H.E.R., "Is he enough?" Complete silence. My husband and I were looking at her, and my son looked at her; she did not respond. I figured he would not marry her, but a few days later, he let me know they had been married since May.

On their wedding day. I arrived at the venue, which was a mansion. One of the rooms, where the bridesmaids would be, was decorated with Chanel décor. The groomsmen were downstairs, and they had a bowling alley. I was isolated on the other end of the house, not benefitting from any of the things that most bridal parties do in preparation for the wedding. I recall the mother and sister, along with the bride, presenting me with a monogrammed blanket a few hours before the wedding. The sister had her phone camera ready as though this was a production, as I have learned most things are with them.

Nothing can be natural. The sister seemed disappointed because my reaction was not grandiose. I was a bit irritated because I knew the wedding would be starting soon, and I hadn't been provided with a space to get ready. Finally, the bride motioned that it was okay for me to get ready. She had provided a make-up artist for the ladies. I was the last one to receive makeup, 10 minutes before the wedding. The artist was working with me in a small entryway to the grand room; it was the size of a small shoe closet. The bridal party was passing through this space to go to the foyer because the wedding was about to begin. I felt so discarded and used. This venue was $10,000, and I was treated with such disdain and disrespect. I hid my true feelings inside to avoid ruining the presentation of perfection. People can show you whatever they want; it is how they make you feel that matters most.

The production was about to begin. Everything was so beautiful. Everyone was playing their respective roles. My father was there, as were my aunts and uncles, his paternal grandfather, and aunts and uncles from his biological father's side of the family. Also present were his friends from college. There was some silent betting on whether the marriage would last more than a year. Her father officiated at the wedding, when he asked, "Does anyone know of any reason why these two people should not be joined in marriage? Speak now or forever hold your peace." On the inside, I was yelling, yes! I do! But what difference would it make since they were already married?

Our son was selected to participate in one of the most challenging law enforcement academies in the United States. During that time in our country, it was not popular to be in law enforcement; however, our son thought he could educate our community and make a difference as a Black male. During his first or second week at the Academy, he was abused by H.E.R. When he shared this with his father and me, we told him to tell someone in leadership whom he trusted what was going on. He said, "What do I look like as a male cadet telling them my wife is beating up on me? They will not believe me."

We insisted that he tell someone. It needed to be documented. He had not listened to us very much in the past, but we later learned that he had listened to us in this regard. Many abusers don't stop abusing unless they do the work to address their sick behavior. As one continues to heal from an abuser, they begin to share all the things they endured because it is a part of them breaking free from what they suffered.

Our first grandson was born in February of 2021. He was approximately 15 months old when more spitting and hitting occurred. My son had been with the police department for two years at that time. There is zero tolerance for domestic abuse, as it should be. He decided he had had enough. He told her he wanted a divorce; he could not go through with it any longer. She kicked him out of the home, and he was forced to live in his car. Three days later, he reached out to me and his father to let us know what was going on, and my heart broke. I was aware that she was pregnant with their second child and thought maybe she was experiencing some hormonal imbalance. It is not our place to make decisions for him; however, this certainly was not an environment conducive to raising children. My fear as a mother was that someone would get hurt, whether it was her hurting him, which we already knew was happening, or him hurting himself. There was nothing in me that ever believed that he would hurt their child.

I was traveling to Dallas for an event, which would also give me a chance to check on my son. When I saw him, my heart broke. He picked me up from the airport in the car he had been living in. I asked him how long he had been living in his car. "Five days," he said woefully. He would shower at the precinct. Before arriving, I told him he needed to withdraw half of the money from their joint checking account so that he could find a place to stay. By the time he had gone to the bank, she had drained the account. She had removed $78,000! How did we get here with H.E.R.? He said he was running out of cash but still stopped by my favorite fast-food restaurant and bought me something to eat. That's how his heart is.

You may say there is no way you would allow someone to treat you this way. You may be one of those who say people must like being mistreated! You must like being abused! That person must have low self-esteem. Those are all the things you should never say to someone who has survived domestic abuse. My son survived domestic abuse as a child, and he was being retraumatized as an adult. A few years ago, I was told that if you can identify a negative, generational spirit, you can break its curse. I thought I had until our family experienced H.E.R.

During devotion one morning, the Lord dropped the word 'Jezebel' into my spirit. I thought, *Jezebel, why are you sharing this word with me now?* I was reading the Word, specifically the book of Revelation, with my sister. While following the guidance of the Holy Spirit and revisiting the story of Jezebel, I learned she was manipulative, deceitful, and did not concern herself with how others felt. She was only worried about her needs and how they could be met. She demanded complete compliance, refused to accept blame for anything, and took credit for everything, as if it made her look good. She was vengeful when confronted. She was cunning and transactional in her approach to others. As I began to sit with what I was discovering about Jezebel and reflected on our experiences with H.E.R., as I mentioned before, when you can identify the spirit you are wrestling with, you can break the generational curse. When you recognize your enemy, you can fight it effectively. How different things could have been if this revelation had come sooner. Being removed from the circumstances that disrupted the balance in your life, you can reflect and experience a clearer vision. I know that it is easy to say what one should have done; however, there is a psychological paralysis that occurs when you are living in a toxic, traumatic environment.

While in town, I reached out to her to let her know that I would only be in the area for a short time, and I wanted to see my grandson. It is always a game with her, and nothing is ever easy. It is almost like walking through a minefield, one wrong step and boom! You may or may not get your desired outcome, and that includes seeing my first grandson. It saddens my heart that I am unable to experience the natural joy of what most grandparents get to experience every day. To be the first great-grandchild for my father, and he also cannot experience what I yearn for daily. Due to time constraints, I reached out to her mother. She was not happy with me for doing that. Having control is especially important to H.E.R. My son and I went to her mother's home, which was part of the regular visitation plan. I could never take my grandson anywhere. I always had to see him at her mother's or her home, and I was always supervised. I later discovered that I was, in fact, being watched. They had a baby camera in the room. They did not trust me to be alone with my grandson because of something my son shared with H.E.R.

She believed that while I was a graduate student and working a full-time and part-time job, and my sons were in the care of their father, I failed to protect them. Our son shared that with his wife, explaining an attempt by a young girl who tried to touch him when he was at his cousin's home with his father. Our son shared that he had never been molested; however, she distorted the story. In her mind, if I could not protect my children, how could I defend hers? I had to learn that during a divorce proceeding. Not once did they ever share their concerns. They pretended and gave the appearance of normalcy. At the same time, they were gaslighting me the entire time.

During my next visit to Texas, following their separation, I spoke with H.E.R.'s mother and arranged a time for us to see the baby. My son and I arrived to find an agitated atmosphere. The father was not home. The mother was acting as though my son had not been away from his son for several days. She was making small talk. Her son and his girlfriend were there. My son's wife was very dry, disrespectful, and rude. I remained calm because I was finally able to hold my grandson in my arms. Typically, when you close out your stay, the mother has a way of cornering you and asking questions as you are leaving. I had already made up my mind that if she asked me how I was doing, I was going to tell her the truth. When she asked me, I responded by saying I was not doing well at all. "I am tired of your daughter putting her hands and her bodily fluids on my son." By this time, we were at her front door. My son had gone to their garage to put a license plate on his vehicle. Her daughter walked in between us to walk out the front door while we were talking.

The mother said to me, "He knows that he can stay here with us."

I replied, "You really think he would be comfortable staying at the parents' home of his abuser?"

Her daughter walked back into the house and growled, "Bitch, what did you say?"

I told H.E.R., "I am talking to your mother, so please go outside."

H.E.R.'s mother also pleaded with her to go outside. She came back in and called me a "bitch" again. I looked at her mother and said, "I wondered when she, the real H.E.R., was going to show up." As I walked outside, she called me a "bitch" for the third time. My son heard her as he was coming from the garage, walking up the driveway, and inquired, "What did you call my mother?"

One thing I know about both of my sons is how they feel about me. They will not let anyone disrespect me. That was a day that I will never forget. I have never had anyone other than my ex-husband speak to me in the manner that she did. While pregnant with our second grandson, she tried to fight me. Her brother had to place her over his shoulder to impede her ability to get to me. Because she had a Victim Protection Order (VPO) against her for hitting a woman in the back of the head the year prior, I knew what she was capable of doing. I turned my back on her in hopes that she would hit me. Her mother was yelling at her to go into the house.

"You must be proud of yourself for the type of men you raised, "she yelled at me while proclaiming what a horrible mother I was and swore to me that I would never see my grandsons.

My son was talking to the mother on the front porch, pleading, "I came to you for help. You knew she was beating me, and you did nothing."

The mother's response was, "What did you expect me to do?"

"I expected you to talk to her, to help us," he lamented.

By this time, I see my grandson looking at us while in his uncle's girlfriend's arms, and his eyes are as big as saucers.

"Let's go!" I looked at my son. "Don't do this in front of your son. Let's go. They are not listening to you. They don't see you. Let's go."

As we were walking away, she continued bellowing hurtful, ungodly things, and I threw my hand up. The mother immaturely commented to H.E.R., "She just threw her hand up. She is done with you, girl."

It was at that moment that I realized the mother was, and still is, just as messy. For a child to be a narcissist, they have to have a narcissistic parent(s). A narcissist is not born; they are taught. For so long, I thought it was the father. It was the mother. There is so much our family is enduring because of her inability to feel; however, this is a story for our son to share when he is ready.

What I will say about being the mother of an adult African American man who has survived an abusive relationship is this: It is heartbreaking to watch your son lose pieces of himself trying to love someone who keeps breaking him. It is painful not being able to fix a situation for your child. It is even more difficult when they have to choose their life over remaining in a situation that is draining life out of them. It is distressing to watch them try to heal the problem yet struggle with the knowledge that nothing they do is right. It is exhausting. Imagine deciding to stay for your kids, doing what is right to be a good father, while being a public servant dedicated to protecting the citizens in your city, and not being respected behind your badge.

Getting verbally and sometimes physically assaulted while at work and being dehumanized and assaulted by your wife when you come home. Do you stay for the children, or do you save yourself so you will be alive to see your children later? What people do not understand about being in an abusive relationship with a narcissist is that no one wins. You will never get it right with them. I know you can go to marriage counseling to learn better communication skills. This certainly works when both parties accept accountability for their part in their madness. Narcissists cannot own their part because if their partner did what they were told to do, all would be well. These actions are not limited to the spouse; they extend to the family. This woman has disrespected our family in so many ways that it is a game to her. She is using our grandsons as pawns, as she knows this is the one thing in the world we care about more than anything, and withholding them causes us pain.

My son left the marriage because it was unhealthy. Leaving his ex-wife did not mean he did not want to have a relationship with his sons. They need both of their parents. It is truly so sad to see someone break because they want to be a father to their boys, yet you have a woman who gaslights and plays games every time. I recall a time when H.E.R. said my son was being abusive. It was hard for me to believe. I will say that I have good discernment when it comes to recognizing when a woman has been abused. Still, I know that no one is perfect, and anyone can be pushed to their limit. My sons and I made a pact that no matter what, they would never hit a woman.

I watched a reality show featuring H.E.R. and my son play out. Yes, a reality show. Image is that important to H.E.R. Everything is a production. It was all about views and displaying the perfect image on social media when chaos was occurring behind the scenes- another characteristic of a narcissist. The reality show was titled "Good Sex," and aired only for one season on the Discovery Channel. When my son mentioned they were going to be on the show, I thought he was joking. He didn't want to do it, but it was something she wanted to do, and he thought it might even help their marriage. I decided to watch the show.

My first thought was, did H.E.R.'s father have any idea that she did the show, considering his religious position? There was one scene where she mentioned that she wanted him to be more aggressive. She wanted him to grab her by the neck in the bedroom. I could not believe my ears. In my intimate partner violence survivor's mind, I thought the last thing a woman who has been abused wants is for her spouse or significant other to be aggressive in the bedroom. There was another episode where she identified the things that she wanted from my son, but then, when he did them, she accused him of being a pedophile. When the show's sex therapist countered that he did what she asked for, she became upset. The therapist told her, "Do you know what you want? When you are confused and unsure of what you want, it is difficult to be in a relationship with someone else, especially when the line of expectation is always changing."

While in divorce court, I recall a video being played. I could hear my son saying, "Stop hitting me. Stop hitting me." His ex-wife was playing a video for the court because she said my son hit her. I sat in the back of the courtroom with my sister, questioning if my son was an abuser. For the first time, I second-guessed our pact never to hit a woman no matter what. When I talked to the lawyer, I asked her and my son if he had hit H.E.R. I told them both, if you did, "I will beat your ass right here in this hallway." His attorney explained he did not hit H.E.R. and that her video exhibit was more damaging to her case because she was the aggressor. She further explained, "Your son was behind a door and was able to shut the door on her, but he did not hit her."

I would be lying if I said the destruction of this union doesn't hurt my heart because it does. As evil as she and her family have been to our family, I still pray for them. I pray for our grandsons, whom we don't get to see. The narrative is that it is our fault. We moved away. "You can see them whenever you want." This all sounds great, right? The reality is that it is a fight just for my son to talk to them on the phone, let alone see them. There is no co-parenting with a narcissist unless you can enforce the court order. So off to court again he will have to go. However, when she was trying to whoop my behind, she said I would NEVER see them again. She is currently making sure that does not happen.

When it is time, we will use the court system to fight for our ability to see our babies. The most excellent lawyer I know is God, and I know He keeps receipts. I understand how He cares for me and what is attached to me. I have given it to God. I realize I cannot fix this, but I am connected to the One who can. My grandsons need both their parents and their paternal family in their lives. One day, we will be able to experience the gift of these blessings. I desire that no family has to experience the pain we are experiencing. I hope that our scars will be the roadmap to someone else's healing and perhaps prevent them from entering into a toxic relationship in the first place because they will recognize the signs.

REFLECTION QUESTIONS:

1. What kind of conversations are you having with your sons, and what kind of questions are you asking to inform them that they should be aware of women who are trying to change the core of who they are?

....

....

....

....

....

2. When meeting your son's potential mate, ask the tough questions. Ask them, "What is it about my son that you appreciate? Is he enough? Is it safe for him to be vulnerable with you? What does it mean to you to create a space of vulnerability for a man? Do you want a soft life? What does it mean to you to have a soft life?

....

....

....

....

....

....

3. Do you know the signs of a narcissist?

BAG LADY

"Come to me, all you who were weary and burdened, and I will give you rest. Take my yoke upon you and learn from me, for I am gentle and humble in heart, and you will find rest for your souls. For my yoke is easy and my burden is light." Matthew 11:28-30 (NIV)

A backpack, diaper bag, handbag, lunch bag, feeling the weight of each while I try to balance life, work, husband, kids, and everything that is thrown at me. I can do it. I got it. This is how I maneuvered through life. I am a strong Black woman! I didn't realize my strength lies in my calmness. My strength is in my ability to say no. My strength lies in my complete reliance on God. My strength lies in not feeling responsible for the weight of others. However, before coming to this realization, I would not seek or depend on anyone else because I did not want to owe anyone anything. I did not want them to throw back in my face what they had done for me. I learned not to depend on others at a young age. I learned that others will disappoint you, and if they are willing to help you, it will come at a cost. Helping them is a transactional, conditional arrangement, not one based on your need for help. Their help is about what you can do for them. Even those who say they love you.

I found it hard to trust because I would give so much of myself so many times, and my heart would be broken time and again. I have carried the baggage of my mother's pain, her mother's pain, and that of anyone willing to allow me to take theirs, because I genuinely believed that it was my burden to bear. I had conditioned myself to carry the emotional weight of others, so that even in my travel and daily work routine, I was literally holding all the things. I was heavy, my back hurt, my neck hurt, and my bra straps dug into my skin from the weight of the various bags I was carrying. I viewed it as being prepared, making sure I had what I needed packed and tucked away, and always mindful that someone else may have needed something I had.

These bags were like my security blanket. How could I be secure with the weight of things that sometimes felt as though they were suffocating me? I would never leave home without my bags. What is crazy is that if I unintentionally left one behind, I would go back and pick it up even if I didn't need it. Thinking I might need it, pushed me to retrieve it. When I began to unpack and heal, I slowly let go of what I was carrying. I realized the pain that I was carrying was not mine. It was my mother's inability to forgive. The bitterness she had embraced as though it were something not worth letting go.

The sadness she stored as though it were as precious as her many adorned jewels. If she had sustained the pressure that comes with healing, she would be the jewel to be adorned. The baggage of her mother hid within her shame. Failing to address family secrets that harmed relationships, silenced voices, and buried pain became baggage. Who would have the courage to let go of the baggage stand and say, "This is not mine!"? Who could say, "This belongs to you," as they returned the baggage to its rightful owner

From one generation to the next, we have carried anxiety, fear, discouragement, complacency, poverty mindset, lack of trust, domestic violence, and damaged relationships. All because it was too hard to do the work to heal. We were taught not to be vulnerable, not to share our personal family business with others, and to give the appearance of being happy and whole, instead of getting down and dirty with what made us feel so ugly. It has taken some time, but I have finally become tired and have witnessed the personal damage of what fighting not to heal looks like. This generational trauma trend stops with me. I will bear the pain and carry the baggage of healing. I will be restored and renewed so that my legacy will not have to bear the burden of the worn luggage I have.

I have decided to unpack every bag that I have carried for so long and pick up peace, develop healthy boundaries, and affirm myself with the words that God breathed into me. I have decided to walk in the boldness of God's power and the stillness of His grace. I now know that I am fearfully and wonderfully made, and I was not made to exist in a defeated posture but to stand tall without picking up baggage that has never belonged to me. The only bags I carry now are those that hold the contents of purchases made from the finest designer stores or the necessities to nourish my soul. What baggage are you holding on to? Are you willing to let go of what is weighing you down and stifling your posture? What I want now is to dwell so much in God that I get lost in His peace, and unbothered by all the things that (by society standards) should bother me.

How do you surrender the things that you have carried for so long? You let go. You surrender, completely trusting God. Think of any relationship you have been in with someone. What did they have to do for you to trust them? Perhaps you asked them to take you to your favorite destination. If they did this more than once, you begin to feel that you can trust them. You can depend on them to be on time and to safely transport you. If you lend your friend money and they repay you as promised, you are more likely to help them again. If you can trust a friend at their word, why can't you trust God with His?

One day, as I was leaving a meeting, I saw a fellow attendee who was weighed down by a backpack. It was so heavy that the thread in the seams was stretching from the strap. She was carrying a stainless-steel cup, a heavy tote bag, and something that appeared to be a folding chair. The Lord said, "Help her."

I walked over to her and said, "Sis, let me take some of this."

She politely said, "I have it."

I responded, "I know you do. But let me lighten your load."

She was nicely persistent, "Oh, you don't have to, I have it."

These are many of the things I would say when someone is trying to help me. So, I persisted. I shared with her, "The Holy Spirit said to help you. Now, do you want me to disobey God?"

She began to relinquish one of the items but would not let go of the backpack. I walked her to her car, which was in the opposite direction from where I was parked. It was a struggle for her to let go of her baggage to allow someone to lighten the load. God wants to lighten our load. He wants to give us rest, but we have to surrender the load to Him. To let go of what is weighing us down. I no longer wish to be a bag lady. I no longer want to carry what is not intended for me. Consider the questions asked throughout this chapter, reflect on them, and think about how you can release the weight you have accepted and carried as your own.

THE MAN WHO STRENGTHENED US. MY KING

"Her husband has full confidence in her and lacks nothing of value." Proverbs 31:11(NIV)

I did not meet him at my best. I met him while still trying to piece myself back together after eleven and a half years of emotional, psychological, and physical abuse inflicted by my ex-husband. I was prepared to be a single mother, raising two Black boys, although this is not what I wanted for them. But then came you. My heart was still bruised. My boys were watchful, quiet, learning how to read a room for safety instead of joy. When you came into our lives, you didn't try to fix us. You made space for me, for us to breathe. I had this independence that mistakenly led me to believe I didn't need anyone. At times, I may have made you feel like I didn't need you or your help. I had to do everything on my own for so long that I would not ask you for anything. I vowed that I would never be in a situation where I would lose my sense of self again, as I did while married to my ex-husband. That I would not allow myself to become so bankrupt psychologically, emotionally, and financially. It was almost as though I were that little girl again. Asking my father for shoes, and remembering how dismissed, unloved, and insignificant I felt by the man that I saw as my provider.

So, for many years, through my healing, I may have made you feel unappreciated, not needed for financial support, because I am that independent woman. The mentality that I do not require you beyond your presence and safety. I am not the same woman. I have healed. I have matured and realized I need you to surprise me by leaving some spending money on my nightstand or by giving me "I was just thinking of you" gifts. Random acts of kindness are my love language. I now realize that your love has never been conditional. I don't have to worry about owing you if you do something nice for me because you love me, no matter what.

Before meeting you, I had learned how to live with tension - constantly feeling like I was in fight or flight mode. My body constantly felt anxious and afraid. I was always expecting the worst, as it seemed to be the only outcome I could expect. Honestly, it is what I expected. To expect something different always led to disappointment. Often, I felt this was what I deserved for making a decision that impacted my sons. The shame. The inability to trust others, always feeling that anyone I encountered had a hidden agenda. No one just wanted to be in my space for me. It was for what they could receive, as if all of this was normal. I didn't even notice the way I held my breath around men. How my heart would race, and my palms would sweat. I always felt someone was going to yell, hit, or spit on me for something I said or did. I constantly felt like I was walking on eggshells. I felt this way in my home, at work, and wherever I went. Long after leaving my abuser, I still held these feelings. Some may say you rescued me, and maybe there is some truth to that. It wasn't a fairy tale kind of rescue. You didn't swoop in with armor. Your armor was how you showed up. We talked for about two months before we met. You were patient.

You listened without judgment. You held space for my story without trying to rewrite it. I waited several months before you met the boys, and I remember you buying what they needed, not what you thought they wanted. You brought groceries. You bought their first pair of Air Force Ones, which began their love affair with sneakers. Shoes have become a fetish of ours. I remember all the years my boys could only have one good pair of shoes because there wasn't any money for others. Sometimes, still wearing shoes they had outgrown, but then came you. You were caring for them long before you met them.

While we were dating, you asked, "Why did I stay?" You were referencing my staying in an abusive marriage for several years. "I would have left a long time ago. I would never be with someone who treated me that way." This is a question that is often asked, and sadly, it is one that is clearly understood by those who have lived it. What I am most thankful for with you is that, although you did not understand and could not fathom the thought of this being a daily existence, when we decided to become a family, you created a home of safety for the boys and me. You loved them as your own. It seems the boys felt this love as well.

One day, after we had been married for two years, we picked the boys up from school. We stopped by the gas station to fuel up.

While waiting to fill up the car, we were talking about the boy's day at school. During the conversation, our oldest blurted out, "Dad, may I have your last name?"

I looked at you, my husband, and you looked at me. I then asked our son, "Why do you want to change your last name?"

He responded, "Because I do not want to be associated with failure."

I don't know how you felt at the time; however, we discussed his request later that evening. You shared how honored you were that he wanted your name. You also shared how you did not want to be disrespectful to another Black man and did not feel their biological father's rights should be severed, but you would happily do a name change. After we talked, I put on my attorney hat and went to the law library to learn how to file an order for a name change. After filing the appropriate forms and legal proceedings, a date was set. I remember that day like it was yesterday. We were all dressed in our Sunday best as we stood before a judge, and in a matter of minutes, we all had the same last name.

It has not always been easy. My healing has not been linear. Some days I felt whole; other days I felt afraid. But you never shamed the process. When I needed silence, you gave it to me. When I needed honesty, you spoke it. Slowly, with you by my side, I stopped flinching at kindness and at love. You truly demonstrated to me what true love looks like. I have always been able to be exactly who I am, while trying to rediscover these lost parts of me. You helped me to believe again, in love, in safety, and most importantly, myself. You also taught me how to speak my mind unapologetically.

Today, I am so thankful for the amazing man you have been. I can witness all the love and time you have poured into both of our sons. They are not perfect by any means; however, they are better with you than without you. They are both college graduates because of you. They have both been on the right side of the law by being servant leaders that any parent would be proud of.

What I love about you the most is your sense of humor. There isn't a day that goes by without you making me laugh. I have been laughing at you, and with you, for twenty-one years. You have seen both the worst and the best of me. I have laughed every day. Although I am still healing. You remain. You have been a vital part of showing me unconditional love. There are still so many things that creep into my soul, but with you, you show gentleness and so much kindness. You have been so patient with me. The Bible says, "Love is patient, love is kind. It does not envy, it does not boast, it is not proud. It does not dishonor others, it is not self-seeking, it is not easily angered, it keeps no record of wrongs. Love does not delight in evil but rejoices with the truth. It always protects, always trusts, always hopes, always perseveres. Love never fails" (1 Corinthians 13:4-8 NIV). We have not always been perfect, but you have always been these things to me. You have never called me out of my name. Maybe under your breath when I have gotten on your last nerve, but never to my face. You have never raised your hand to me. You have never disrespected me. You have never spat on me. You have been the same loving man I spoke to for the first time on the phone. You have shown me, and our sons, what a healthy relationship looks like. You have taught me to use my words to articulate what I need from you. You may not always understand, but in your own time, you listen and provide me with what I need.

We have dreamed together. We have done things scared together. Do you remember when we did the sea walk together in Mexico? You cannot swim at all, and while I can swim, I cannot do it well enough to save both of us. We were on a couple's vacation with extended family. Because I had to work the day before, you didn't participate with the family; you waited so we could experience it together.

I was so afraid of that sea walk. You never said it was eighteen feet deep. What you didn't know is that I had prayed to God about letting go of fear. I asked Him that the next time a fearful opportunity presented itself, to help me face it, knowing He was by my side. I certainly did not expect the opportunity to present itself so soon. It was quite the process to even get to the largest amusement park in the Riviera Maya. I began to talk myself out of the adventurous excursion by telling you all the reasons why we shouldn't do it.

Then you asked, "Didn't you tell your students yesterday that if they were afraid of something, to do it scared anyway?" I wondered, *did this man use my words against me?* It was at that point that I realized there was no turning back.

We walked through the amusement park, enjoying the surroundings as we made our way to the sea walk. Once we arrived, we watched a video that explained the apparatus we would wear on our heads and how we would walk on the sea floor. When our group was called, it was time for me to face my fear, and you were right behind me. I felt supported, but I could also feel fear. I began to pray and fully trust God. When I let go and allowed myself to enjoy what we were experiencing together, I had the most fantastic time. We did it! We did something scary together. Entirely out of the box for both of us. That experience will resonate with me forever. I was ready for our next adventure. It is an experience I will never forget.

We have played "the dozens" for years, cracking jokes on each other in fun, and in the beginning, I was horrible at it. In finding myself, I learned to think quickly on my feet because the trauma endured had silenced my thoughts and caused me to freeze at any familiarity with a threat. You continued to play with me until I became stronger and more confident as I began to heal through so many years of smallness.

In some ways, I walk through the healing journey with my clients. The more exposure you have to something and realize it is not a threat, the more relaxed your mind becomes, and you can move and think more freely. That is how it has been with you as we laugh and joke with one another. Now that I have perfected this craft, I can hang with you, and we keep each other cracking up.

We fell in love with each other, not based on appearance, although we both say we "upgraded" one another, but by our hearts. You have been everything that I needed. You have consistently demonstrated self-assuredness about yourself, creating an atmosphere that supports the idea that we can achieve anything if we believe in ourselves and work hard. I have always felt so safe with you. You have always encouraged me to make my own decisions and given me space to be my own person outside of our relationship. I have never felt smothered by you because of your self-assurance. You have been the polar opposite of my former relationship. I know God sent you to me because I listened to His voice this time. My spirit chose you before anything in my carnal being could. I am thankful that you chose us. As we continue to age together, I pray for our health and that we will continue to laugh and do all the crazy things until the wheels fall off while we sing, "Ooh la la la!"

DEAR SONS

"Correct thy son, and he shall give delight unto your soul." Proverbs 29:17 (KJV)

I am not sure when I decided I wanted to have a child, given that many decisions at that time in my life were based on what was going to bring peace and not further destruction in my marital relationship. I was only twenty-three years old when I became pregnant the first time. I had no idea what it meant to be a wife, let alone a mother. Perhaps, something in me reasoned, the disgust he saw in me would magically disappear if I bore him a child. Not realizing at the time that he was more disgusted with himself and projected all his hate for himself onto me. It was naive to believe that having a child would help restore my being and our relationship.

How could I put so much hope in the innocence of a child to bear the weight of my pain? He wanted you. I was scared to have you. I didn't know if I could care for you. If I could protect you from his unstable behavior, since I was unable to defend myself. There were so many things I was afraid of when becoming a mother. But perhaps I would have someone who would love me unconditionally, someone I could care for and be there for in ways my mother wasn't there for me.

It is unbelievable that I began to think like so many women. That having a child would improve my life and my relationship. One thing was indeed true: you improved my life and saved it at the same time. Words cannot adequately express the love that I have for both of you. There have been moments in life that are too heavy for children to carry, yet you both have witnessed more than I ever wanted your eyes to see and your minds to retain.

Carrying the images of what we lived through is not something that can easily be erased. I have grieved for many years over the pain that you witnessed me go through, never wanting either one of you to be prey or prey on others. More than anything, I want you to know that you are not defined by those moments. Do not allow anyone or anything to tell you otherwise. What defines you is God's love, His strength, and the courage that I see in both of you each day. You defied the odds.

My two baby boys. My heart. My 'son-shines,' brightening up my day and keeping me in the world, because I wanted you both to have so much more than I was able to give. I wanted you to know what unconditional love looked like. I wanted you to know that working hard pays off, that you are enough to be loved right where you are, and that God's love can love you to your destiny. I wanted you to love your queen in ways that would make her feel safe and worry-free. That you and she would support each other and that she would not change you into what she wanted you to be, but what God designed you to be. I recently attended a pottery workshop, which reminded me of God's presence with us. He can take a piece of clay (you and me), He will mold this clay, and even with our imperfections, He will add water (the Word) to help smooth out the edges. While applying a little pressure, it will make what has tried to fracture us disappear. What one could visibly see is no longer there. Once God has formed us and smoothed us out, we are unbreakable. As long as we remain connected to Him, He will continue to pour into us all that we need.

There are definitely some things I regret, and one of them will never be either one of you. Had I made different decisions, you would not have been here. I do believe what was right about the church saying your biological father was my husband, so that I would have both of YOU in this world. All that we have experienced is to be shared to help bring someone else to healing and wholeness while we continue to work through our pain. The beauty of life is that we have the opportunity to choose how we will live with the life we have been blessed to have. When I look at both of you, I am given the strength to be exactly what God designed for me to be. I am so proud of both of you for how you have maneuvered through life. I know it has not always been easy, yet you continue to demonstrate God's love in how you treat others, no matter how hard it is when others mistreat you. Neither of you is perfect. No man is. We are all flawed. Have you made unfavorable choices? An astounding YES! Some have been very costly and painful, BUT GOD! I believe we all have made decisions that have not presented us in the best light; however, what we do with those decisions is to improve our lives. Do we wallow in pain or blame others, or do we lean into what is causing us pain and do our introspective work? The heart work, the uncomfortable work, is necessary for us to grow and break free from what is keeping us bound.

Both of you are my heartbeats. You are the reason I dared to leave such a toxic marriage. I was unable to do it for myself; however, you both gave me the strength to do it for you. Even in the toughest of times, I was able to dig deep within myself because I never wanted to disappoint you. I wanted to give you all the things I was unable to receive from my mother. Your silliness, your inquisitive, thought-provoking questions, and your presence have been my life source. I pray that you always know that I will always love you no matter what. No matter what storms come, we are stronger together. You are brothers, and my greatest joy is for you to stay connected and be there for one another. I want more than anything for you to remain close and be each other's keeper.

To my Caleb: I have watched the way you have carried weight that was not intended for you to carry and maintained a strong demeanor, so you do not appear weak. You are a protector at your core, and your heart desires to honor and protect those you love. But I want you to know that it is not your job to carry someone else's pain. It is okay to be vulnerable, to ask for help, and to let others weather the storm with you and sometimes for you. Your strength shines brightly; however, your gentleness is just as valuable.

To my Cameron: I see your tender spirit behind the tough, I give zero f**cks exterior. I know the way your heart feels deeply. You remind me that love is powerful and being true to who you are is loving yourself and others. Your gentleness has its own kind of courage. Never lose the light that resides within you. You do not have to harden yourself to be safe. You are enough exactly how you are.

My heartbeats: I cannot change what has occurred in the past. Still, I can promise you that I will continue to surround you with love, provide the assurance that you can always confide in me without judgment, and that we will spend time laughing and creating new memories together, rather than dwelling on the past. The past was never your fault. What happened to me, what happened to us, was never due to your existence, but our escape had everything to do with you. I will forever be grateful to you for the courage you gave me to choose us over fear.

Always remember that you are deeply loved, not only by me and your bonus Dad, but by God who created you for greatness. It is by the grace of God that both of you are the strong, intelligent, loving, empathetic men that you are. No matter how hard the devil came for you, he could not win because God had His hand on you the entire time. He will continue to carry you and propel you forward boldly into your purpose.

With all my love,

Mom

REFLECTION QUESTIONS:

1. What is the most important lesson you have learned about life that you should share with your children?

2. What is your greatest concern regarding your child becoming an adult? Have you given this concern to God? Consider finding a scripture in the Bible and stand on this scripture regarding this concern.

3. List your takeaways from this chapter.

DEUCES FEAR

"For God hath not given us the spirit of fear, but of power, and of love, and of a sound mind." ~ 2 Timothy 1:7 (KJV)

As a teenager, I heard a sermon by a well-known evangelist on the topic of fear. He said the word fear stood for False Evidence Appearing Real. Something about this acronym stood out to me. The very existence of what I was afraid of was an impostor. It had not been authenticated; it was a false sense of reality. How can something feel so real yet lack validity? As I reflect on my life and the decisions I have made, I've realized many of my decisions were based on fear and not faith—choices made from my pain. The idea or message came from lived experiences. With not enough positive interactions to support my worth, I walked into believing that I may not be good enough.

Holding on to the meaning the pastor shared, I grew up with the concept of what I believed fear to be. I had many occurrences in my life to deem the concept proper. The reality of fear being something to cripple me, not equip me. An emotion intended to harm me, not protect me. For so many years, fear was the intimidator; it was the THING, the feeling that would keep me from belting out a song in front of others, fearing their chattering would not be affirming to my ego. Not approaching the cute boy in fear of rejection. Not advocating for myself in fear that my voice would be dismissed. In each of these examples, illuminate the anticipated adverse outcomes of fear. Should those anticipated negative outcomes occur, then it simply reinforces your thought to be true. It is no longer a thought; it becomes your reality. Never once considering the gift of what fear brings.

Being Black has come with fear. Keeping us stuck, silenced, and skeptical, as fear was often instilled in us. Should you rise and fight your offender or simply just be you, being black could endanger you to become a strange fruit. Strange fruit is a haunting metaphor for the bodies of Black Americans lynched in the South. Lynching was the extrajudicial killing (often by hanging) of primarily Black men and women carried out by White mobs during the late 19th and early 20th centuries. Lynching was used as a tool of terror and control during and after Reconstruction, keeping Black communities in fear.

I don't ever recall fear being a motivator. Something used to protect me or offend; however, what I have discovered is that the very thing God intended fear to be is what our adversary uses to weaponize. As I continue to walk through this process of healing, I have discovered new meanings of an emotion that has a more profound utilization when we see it for what it truly is. The intended physiological use of fear is to give us the awareness of a perceived threat, danger, or harm, whether it is real or imagined. It is a part of our body's survival system. Our bodies prepare us to either confront the threat, escape, or immobilize. All of which demonstrates the intended protective purpose of fear to keep us alert and alive. Fear can also guide us in setting boundaries and recognizing danger. Fear can be like a two-edged sword. It can be both a warning and a prison sentence. When we are consumed with fear, it can cripple us and prevent us from moving forward in our lives. This was never God's intended use of fear. God discusses fear with the intention of releasing us from fear because God promises us strength, peace, and presence. Our adversary promises weakness, unrest, and uncertainty.

I decided to choose God's intended use of fear. Now, this is not a decision that was made overnight. It was definitely a result of trial and error. I was doing things my own way because I was still struggling to trust God. For most of my life, I had to depend on myself, which was sometimes a struggle. What a perplexing place to be when you lack faith in the one who created you and confidence in yourself. When you have lived through trauma, fear is not an abstract feeling; it lives rent-free in your mind and in your body. To conquer fear, but about erasing it, is about reclaiming everything the enemy intended to confiscate—your sense of safety, trust, and most importantly, your faith.

In my efforts to release fear, I first had to acknowledge its existence without judgment. Fear is a dangerous thing. It can be crippling. It can be paralyzing. It can also be the motivator of decisions if you allow it. It can prevent you from moving forward, taking that first step toward your dreams. The steps taken to share this story have been challenging and downright painful because there is still this quiet voice whispering all the reasons why I should not move forward, but God. His voice is overpowering and gives me the strength to move forward despite my feelings. An element of fear and vulnerability has been a consistent presence, stirring up internal procrastination and fear of writing. I found every reason not to sit and write what I have feared. The secret conversations. The thought of another story. What makes your story any different than anyone else's? Girl, everyone is writing a book. All of these thoughts and ideas are judgment.

When my ex-husband placed a loaded gun to my head with his hand on the trigger, in fear, I prayed to God that if He allowed me to live, I would share my story with every person I could to help them escape a life of abuse. Fear prompted me to make a promise to my Creator. That same fear and shame kept me from fulfilling my promise for many years. Fear kept me from revisiting the trauma that I experienced in that marriage. Fear manifested in my jobs, where I could not fully reach my potential because I was afraid of negative feedback and lacked self-confidence. I preferred to be the background music. I learned to be a great supporting cast member and servant to others, but never the one out front. That was not my thing. Being seen was not important to me. I was a great team player, but to lead, not so much. How could I lead when I couldn't even make sound decisions? I had married a man who was whooping my ass before I married him.

Not only did he abuse me physically, emotionally, and psychologically, but I also lay with him and bore two sons. How could my voice be heard in a world full of judgment and criticism? To be out front. That was laughable. That idea vanished after repeatedly being told I lacked worth and was insignificant. He would tell me many times that I wasn't a woman because I carried myself like a little girl. I couldn't make love right. I was a virgin when I married him. I promised God that if I couldn't do anything right, I would save myself for marriage. This is what I did, but I wasn't rewarded. I was punished because I married a man who did not appreciate or understand the purpose of saving myself for my husband. If he did, surely, he would not have abused me.

God created fear as a survival response. To alert our souls of danger, not to consume our souls. After enduring trauma, your nervous system stays on high alert. Our bodies were never intended to function at this level daily. Through our traumatic experiences, our bodies have learned to make fear a permanent residence: no longer an intruder, but a permanent guest. To remove something that you no longer desire, you must first acknowledge it. This is the beginning of loosening the grip of fear.

Once I acknowledged fear, it forced me to feel all the things regarding my violent marriage, which left me feeling unsafe and vulnerable. Many lives were lost during the pandemic that began in 2019; however, this was the beginning of me finding mine when I was forced to sit in my pain and face all of the trauma I had been running from all of my life. I could no longer hide in my work, sports activities, or use retail therapy because the entire world was shut down. At the age of 49 years old, I was sitting in the pain of childhood traumas, marital rape, physical, emotional, and psychological abuse, church trauma, mommy issues, guilt, shame, lack of self-assuredness, impostor syndrome, and the list could go on and on. None of what God says I am; however, I had strayed so far from faith that I was operating under my own might because if no one else had my back, I knew I did. Something I would like to share with you about my healing journey and letting go of fear is that I am in the present. I am no longer in a relationship that makes me afraid of who God has created me to be. My body and nervous system do not have to prepare and protect themselves from an immediate threat, because no threat resides within my home. Now, through practices of mindfulness, grounding exercises, deep breathing, and stretching, my body realizes that I am not in a traumatic moment, but in a peaceful one.

Once you have acknowledged your fear and reconnected with your body, you must find your people. Those beautiful humans who will anchor you. That will help you feel safe and not judge you when you slip back temporarily into those areas of your life that are familiar. Because the enemy will try to remind you of who you once were, instilling fear. Consider an anchor as someone who supports you and affirms you. They remind you of who you are in Christ. My phenomenal mindset coach, Dr. Cheryl Polote-Williamson, affirmed with me on February 13, 2023, that fear is not a factor for me. Her statement became my battle cry. These are the words that awakened my soul.

I have spoken to many women who desire to start a business, go back to school, or pursue a new venture, but will not because they are afraid. Because of this shift within myself, I have encouraged women to look within themselves and explore the very thing that scares them. Once it is identified, ask God what He thinks about the thing, person, or situation you are afraid of. Fear is intended to alert you and protect you, not consume you or inhibit your progression. I encourage you to step out on faith and trust God. When He is for you, who can be against you? When He places the idea or the gift in you to do, He expects you to do it and share it with others to help them heal and experience the love of Christ. This is the enemy's fear. When you understand how the designer built you, you know your purpose and your identity. If you are afraid, do it scared. In "doing it scared," taking that leap of faith, you come to realize that God has carried you the entire way, and He will do it repeatedly until you know that beyond a doubt, He is ALWAYS going to come through for you because He fulfills His promises. However, you won't know His promises if you don't have a relationship with Him.

Gradually, expose yourself to safe risks. This is how you recondition your mind and your body to shrink fear. It is a form of slow surrender. I often remember interacting with H.E.R. or anyone similar to the spirit that resided within H.E.R., and it would agitate that old spirit of intimidation or fear. Your body remembers this feeling. My mind and my faith would be strong; yet my body had not forgotten. I would get so frustrated with myself because I was being weakened, and I was allowing them to win. Not realizing at the time, these gradual exposures would slowly catch up to my faith, meaning God was conditioning me. Although it is highly uncomfortable, it is necessary for your healing. Little by little, I was able to let go of things I could not control and pay attention to the somatic responses my nervous system was signaling to me. Now, when I interact with this demonic spirit, I am not moved by its tactics. I have reclaimed my life by making intentional steps towards the things that once felt frightening. Each success built confidence and increased my faith.

Overcoming fear is really about reclaiming your voice and practicing compassion toward yourself. Conquering fear after trauma is not linear, and some days you are going to feel heavy, but remind yourself that you have survived. You are here for a purpose, and you will walk boldly in that purpose unmuted!

Every day that I am on this earth is a miracle. Every day I breathe because my Heavenly Father has allowed me to see another day to fulfill my purpose. Many days, I would weep because I was unaware of my worth and allowed others to cause me to feel insignificant because I was not doing enough, not pretty enough, not smart enough, simply not enough. God said, "When I died for you on the cross, that's when I determined you were more than ENOUGH!" I was unmuted! My ability to speak freely without shame was slowly emerging. I was fighting mentally and emotionally to find my voice while I healed. I have allowed fear to reside in my mind, in my heart, and in my soul.

I have decided to evict FEAR. It has no place in my life. It can no longer rule and reign in partnership with fear. The Lord has always said that He has not given us the spirit of fear, but of love and a sound mind. What we miss in this scripture is that, like other things not of God, we can pick up or practice things that God has not given us. My heart now receives, and my mind believes this to be true. So, deuces fear! Goodbye to fear and hello to power. I have committed to beginning each day with powerful declarations to remind myself of the things that no longer serve my peaceful soul, and I would like to share them with you.

I declare and decree that today, I am no longer bound by fear, but I am bold and courageous through God's power working in me. I declare and decree that I will lean into my faith, which is greater than fear. I declare and decree that I believe God will strengthen me and uphold me with His righteous hand. I will no longer allow others to attach their narrative of me and wear it as though it is more significant than what God has created me to be on this earth.

Now, it is your turn! Create three declarations of your own to help say deuces to fear and lean into it!

SHATTERING SHAME

"As scripture says, anyone who believes in him will never
be put to shame." Romans 10:11 (NIV)

I have lived, as I mentioned earlier, most of my life making others comfortable, serving them, and helping them fulfill their dreams and purpose. The background was my safe place. At least in the background, my failures are not up front to the world and those looking in to see. In the shadows, I can hide. This is part of the conversation of shame.

In shame, the reminder of a failed marriage resides. For so long, I wore shame like a pair of chic designer frames. A barrier that prevented others from looking into my eyes, the window to my soul. Afraid, they would see the doubt and the guilt that I tried to hide. Shame told me that somehow everything that occurred was my fault. Shame told me I should have known better, left sooner, fought harder. Shame would whisper with gladness that I was weak. The truth was buried so deep within me that I had to dig deep to unearth it through many years of tears and therapy.

Surviving was never a weakness. Surviving was my strength. The enemy intended to destroy me and everything attached to me. Shame was one of his fiercest tactics. Shame discounts your witness and testimony before you can fully find a way to declare it. Shame says, "You do not want to rediscover your worth and who you are in Christ." When I removed my glasses, I was able to reveal myself. I was able to look into the eyes of others, no longer concerned about what might reflect back at me. I began to surrender to the cares of someone else's criticism or judgment. I started to peel away shame, replacing it with compassion for the woman who had endured what God never intended for her to carry. Now, when I look in the mirror, I do not see someone consumed by staying in an abusive relationship or struggling with desiring the love and support of her parents. I see someone empowered.

The very essence of shame is an identity-based wound that depicts itself as "I am wrong," not as "I did something wrong." Often, when clients seek out therapy from me, it is due to grief, a traumatic event, anxiety, depression, or relational conflicts. This may be the presenting packaged issue; however, shame is the underlying issue. Shame is one of the most powerful yet least visible dynamics in psychotherapy. Shame is the felt experience of unworthiness, often internalized from early attachment wounds, some of which I have explored in my own personal life, including critical environments that depict you as not being good enough, as well as cultural and systemic messages. We witness in society daily how those in marginalized populations are less valued. These are all messages received through spoken words and or actions that we believe. The work of shame healing encompasses the separation of identity from experience. Removing internalized messages and creating a space of belonging through safe relational connections. Sometimes it may be challenging to move past what you have done because of what others may think of you or say about you. I have found that people who lack joy will talk regardless. The time we spend worrying about what others think of us could be better spent with those who pour life into us, helping others realize they are not the decision they made. They are not the sum of what happened to them.

In whatever season of life you find yourself in, consider it an opportunity to reflect on things of the past. Reminisce, yes, about what you could have, should have, or wish you had done. But sit in the joy of knowing what has passed, and you are beyond it. Congratulate yourself for not allowing your isms (s), fear, or shame to keep you in pain and darkness. You have moved forward in your life despite the shame that tried to consume you.

If we allow the shame of past decisions, choices, moves, relationships, and denial of self, among other things, to take hold of our being, our voices remain silent. You may not feel that what you have to say matters, or you may fear what someone might say. If they are talking about you, let them talk, because they are going to talk anyway. So, give them something to talk about. Yes, I was married to a man for eleven and a half years who beat me, cursed me, and tried to kill me, but God. But God made a way of escape for me and my sons. He kept His promise to preserve me in a manner that I do not look like what I have been through. Thank God He restores.

When I was a little girl, I remember hearing women sitting around sharing their regrets. Sharing stories of what they wished they had not done. If they had known what they know now, they would have done things differently. An event in their lives that created so much shame they wished it had never happened. What I now realize is that it was giving voice to wisdom. They wanted to share their pain in the hope of preventing similar mishaps from happening to another woman.

Shame will have you sitting in your pain alone, pretending everything is good, not realizing that sharing your experience could be a blessing for someone else. The enemy is clever. If he can keep us silent, fearful, and ashamed, he can keep us from being free. It is okay to acknowledge the fear you are experiencing because it is real, but it is not as real as your faith. If you lean into your fear and trust God, He will consume the fear on your behalf. Here are three steps that helped me shatter shame.

1. Surround yourself with women, sisters who love you and will not allow you to stay stuck in your pain. They'll push you towards your purpose and say what needs to be said,

even if it is something you don't want to hear. It will be the very thing you will need to nourish your soul.

2. Give yourself grace. Believing that all things work together for the good of them who love the Lord. Even when we do what we think is right, outside of God's instructions, He will still work it out to get the glory. He will take our mess and deliver a masterpiece, bringing deliverance for you and someone else.

3. Be obedient. Do what God tells you to do, even when it does not make sense. His plan is always better and greater than what we can imagine. Do not be a negotiator, but an obeyer.

Practice shattering, shattering every emotion, behavior, schism, or belief that holds you in shame. Shattering is defined as the disruption or annihilation of something. Are you ready to shatter, disrupt, and annihilate the shame that exists in your being to create a space for healing and freedom? If so, what will you do to disrupt it, to break the pattern? When you do those things, you will discover the liberation that comes from spreading hope and love within your family, community, and the world. I am thankful for the steps you are willing to take towards YOU.

REMOVING THE MASK

When we remove the veil (a mask) from our faces, we can understand the glory of Christ within us! 2 Corinthians 3:18

According to the Oxford Dictionary, a mask is "a covering for all or part of the face, worn as a disguise, or to amuse or terrify other people" (Oxford University Press, n.d.). One Halloween, as a kid, not understanding the meaning of the night, I was focused on the most essential thing: C-A-N-D-Y! I was permitted to gather as much candy as my heart desired. What I also remember is that I could go to the local T G & Y store and pick out my costume. With each costume came a mask. I could be whoever I wanted to be. From a princess to an evil villain. None of these costumes looked like me. They were not an image of my brown skin, brown eyes, or black hair. However, it afforded me an escape to be someone other than myself for at least one night.

I chose to be a princess. The costume was designed with a light blue, flowy dress, a long, shiny wand, and a mask consisting of pale white skin and bright yellow hair. I guess little White girls were the only princesses in the world. I put on the flowy blue dress, grabbed the wand, and covered my face with the mask that showed what I desired to be as I went from door to door, with a voice of innocence, saying, "Trick or treat."

We learn as children to pretend. To be a superhero that saves the day or pretend to be a teacher or a doctor while playing make-believe. Using our imagination was taught as a healthy form of being. If you see yourself doing something, you can become it. As a child, I never doubted my ability to be whatever I wanted to be, and in many ways, I believe I am exactly where I'm meant to be, thanks to God's will.

From time to time, I have wondered if I had trusted myself instead of believing others were graced with more wisdom than I, would I have still taken the scenic route to my destiny, or the road God had already planned? It is human nature to revisit the land of should have, could have, would have; however, it does not serve us well to do so. Growing up in a home with parents who had their own problems, and again, please understand I love both of my parents; however, having a child when they did was not wise. However, I am sure God was in that, too. I am thankful that they provided me with all they could give. I never experienced hunger in my belly. I lived in a beautiful home and was exposed to various experiences that helped strengthen my character. Yet, I still hungered for their love and attention.

When I was in second grade, my teacher, whom I adored, made me stay after school for, as she put it, "being disruptive." In my opinion, I was honest. Although this was a neighborhood school, I lived far enough away that I had to ride the bus to get there. I didn't have the option of walking home. There was this little boy named KH, who was light-skinned, had green eyes, and was tall for his age. I really thought he was the cutest boy in our class, if not in the entire school. He always made me laugh. I am not sure what he thought about me; however, after that day, he probably thought I was weird.

Our teacher was facilitating a discussion about our favorite things. She led with the question, "What is your favorite vegetable?"

I raised my hand and with confidence I said, "Onion, Mrs. W. My favorite vegetable is an onion."

KH said, "Onion?! Girl, I bet you smell like onions." The class roared.

I was being honest, but the class erupted in loud laughter. When Mrs. W lost control, she had me and KH stay after school to clean the chalkboard. For me, this was terrible. You might as well have given me a death sentence because this meant I would miss the bus. When he was finished cleaning his part of the chalkboard, he walked out of the classroom door and said, "Onions!" And laughed as he walked down the sidewalk. I was so embarrassed. I had to wait for my mother to pick me up. She was not happy. She had to leave work early, so her check would not be her regular earnings. She showed me how upset she was when she pulled out the burgundy belt with the gold buckle. At the age of seven, I received a powerful life message: being honest and being who you are isn't necessarily who you should show others. I put on a mask. I received a beating for telling my truth, was ridiculed in front of my peers, and spanked by my mother because my response inconvenienced her. I began to adapt to my surroundings and be whatever and whomever others wanted me to be.

Not long after this memorable event, I began attending church services not too far from our neighborhood. The joy bus would pick up the little brown kids in the neighborhood and take us to a little city called "The Village." I used to love attending church there because they expressed genuine care for me and my friends. This was my first encounter with Jesus and learning about the books of the Bible. I loved Jesus so much that I gave my life to Him during that time. I was baptized during Vacation Bible School; my parents did not come. I would go every Sunday morning and Wednesday night. My parents would get me ready for church and then go back to bed once they waved me off to catch the yellow and brown joy bus. It looked like a banana, but I looked forward to going each time. We were fed The Word in a fun, engaging manner, and they fed us food. It was such a welcoming place. I was seen and valued. I did not have to pretend to be anyone other than myself.

I became so bold that I began to share the Word with my mother. I wanted to walk in His likeness. I certainly knew I could not be Him; however, I admired Him so much that I found myself trying to live by His principles. My mother was touched by my excitement and decided to attend church with me. I tried to get my father to come, but he decided he would rather attend the church where he was raised. Not a problem. So, we did. The pastor said something my father did not appreciate. I do not recall what it was, but a party of three became a party of two.

From the age of seven to about twelve, I had a strong sense of my identity in Christ. I believed my relationship with Christ was strong. My faith was strong. There was nothing that I did not believe my God could do. As I became older, I lost the sense of this faith due to my interactions with teens and trying to find where I fit in with my peers, because I was always different. I am sure it was due to God living within me. I was making myself small. My teenage self lost her identity in so many ways. I no longer trusted my decisions. I didn't think much of it because most teens don't know who they are and are trying to build up their friend count. We didn't have social media back then, but people were still living their lives for likes, and so was I.

I would mask and conform to whatever situation I was presented with until I reconnected with God around the age of 16 and was intentional again about growing in Christ. There is something about comparing yourself to others, even in the church. I considered myself a baby in Christ, even though I had been talking to God since I was seven years old. I would watch women in the ministry and be fascinated by how they taught or delivered God's Word. They were truly anointed. As I continued to grow in Christ, I thought that at the age of twenty, I had a grasp of where I was in life. There were still some unsettled emotions regarding my parents; however, I thought I was finally returning to discover myself and what I wanted in life. Until I was introduced to him, all the women I admired and respected in the church said the Holy Spirit had said, "He is your husband." I began to compare my spirituality and relationship with others. My prophetic gift had not manifested. So, I doubted what the Holy Spirit had shared with me because it contradicted what they were sharing with me, and I relinquished my confidence, feeling subservient to my spiritual sisters in Christ. Another mask.

A mask that muzzled my voice, so I did not fully trust it. My faith family prayed with my ex-husband and me, and he put on his holy mask and convincingly played the game by going to church and attending Bible studies that would ultimately involve them praying over him to rid him of his ungodly behavior. I always paid a price for his inconvenience. Surviving an abusive relationship has cost me my sense of self. What did I do? I masked up. I found a way to comfortably be something that I was not. To conform or to adapt to any situation. Wearing a mask to pretend that all is well when I was screaming on the inside.

When you become free in Christ and understand His power, you take off the mask and live your life the way He intended for you to live. I started taking steps to remove the mask when my sisters called me out. I knew I was hiding behind what I wore, from my attire to my stylish frames. One day, my trusted sister demanded, "Stop hiding behind your glasses. Let me see your eyes." Funny, I started wearing glasses to help hide the pain in my eyes; now I've become dependent on them to see.

I have been in rooms, and when it was time to introduce myself, I could feel myself cowering and stepping behind other women in a quiet, discreet way. On one occasion, a few of the ladies asked, "Tiffany, are you hiding?" The truth is that other women who care about you can see it no matter how hard you try to hide it, and, if they love you, they will tell you. Although I was beyond embarrassed, because we are all very much grown, business owners for God's sake, I was definitely hiding. Your loving sisters will not allow you to hide, because God didn't design you that way. Acknowledging that you are wearing a mask is the first step. Look at yourself in the mirror, decide to do the heart work, and begin your healing. This looks like sitting in your pain. This involves disconnecting from all the distractions that prevent you from acknowledging what is keeping you from living a fulfilled and healed life. Shut yourself off from others and commune with God. Having a healthy support system around you and accepting the challenge of no longer hiding is the first step in removing the mask. Remember and realize that although weapons will be formed, they will not prosper. I began to explore afresh through God's Word how He sees me. For my heart to truly receive the messages of how and why God created me in His image, I had to take off the garments I had clothed myself in and accept what I was born into.

I had to genuinely believe that I could be my authentic self and be who I was created to be to be truly liberated. I was no longer embarrassed or ashamed by what I had gone through because God brought me through it all. It was then my responsibility to share what He has done for me, so that others could see what is possible. With each opportunity I receive, I give Him glory, whether through my words or simple gestures of love; the mask is being lowered. What I am most grateful for is that the same women who challenged me to remove the mask remain in my life and continue to pour into me when I begin to digress to what is familiar. You must have souls around you who want to see you win and want you to heal. Now, as you heal, some may not be able to handle the healed parts of you, and they will exit. Which is fine, because that is not what you need to thrive and walk boldly in your purpose. So, yes, I was a battered woman, but I am free. Yes, I have broken relationships that I have tried to fix, but only God can repair them. Yes, I have failed. And I have completely taken the mask off! I am free and, quite honestly, I don't care what anyone thinks or what they have to say. I know what God says about me and how He feels about me, and everything connected to me. So, whoever has whatever to say about me, say it! If there is something you want to know, ask me because I would be happy to share how God has set me free! My hope for you is that you will be able to remove your mask and live the life that God so graciously died on the Cross for you to live.

REFLECTION QUESTIONS:

1. What are you masking?

....

....

....

....

....

2. What steps are you willing to take to begin removing the mask?

....

....

....

....

....

3. How do you see yourself? Do you know how God sees you?

....

....

....

....

....

4. Find scriptures that describe how God sees you to help you disrobe from the falsehoods you have clothed yourself with.

....

....

....

....

....

....

....

5. Begin affirming yourself daily by saying the descriptors of who God created you to be.

....

....

....

....

....

....

....

EVERYONE NEEDS A YOU IN THEIR LIFE

"Blessed is she who has believed that the Lord would fulfill His promises to her." Luke 1:45 (NIV)

As we go through life, we need someone on this earth to reassure us that, no matter how we feel or what we are going through, God has our back. One of the most consistent beings in my life has been my sister. Even when my ex-husband isolated me from everyone that mattered, and I no longer had YOU in my life, you did not make me feel bad. YOU embraced me as though I had never left. You understood it was not by choice. We have experienced a certain closeness since I was a child. You were my safe place. You always saw me and only required me to be my best. When I had no confidence, you shared yours until I believed I could do it. You were there every time my mother left my dad. I stayed with you. I was your shadow. I was your little sister. We both had something we constantly desired: a younger or older sibling. I wanted a big sis, and you wanted a little sister, and God gifted us with each other.

I often wondered what my life would have been like if your presence had remained a consistent force. I certainly know that I would not have been in an abusive marriage for as long as I did. You would have been the one to question many of the actions that slowly caused my persona to decay. You would have been the one to help me make sense of what was happening. You would have been able to see through their faux personality from the start. For all of that to exist, it would also mean I wouldn't have my sons. If I had known what I know to be true now, I would have moved differently. However, God had already gone before me and knew what decisions I would make. He made sure that, despite my waywardness, all things would work out for the good.

You have taught me to "use my words" to say what I mean. To create healthy boundaries for myself. YOU have taught me to identify my non-negotiables and not allow others to take advantage of me. To recognize my gifts and stop being the background music. You have taught me that it is okay to be me. To trust God and step out on faith, even when I am scared and fear the worst. Everyone needs a YOU in their life. A sister who does not try to compete but wants you to win. A sister who celebrates your accomplishments. The one who will sit down with you and help you through some of the toughest challenges you may ever face, without judgment, shame, or criticism. You have never said, "If you had listened to me in the first place, you would not have been in this position." You used it as a teachable moment. You have been one of my biggest cheerleaders and my best friend. Whatever hurts my sister hurts me. When my sister wins, I win; we all win. I am grateful for every moment, accomplishment, tear, and laugh we have together. Every person, every woman, every little boy, every little girl needs a YOU in their life.

When I think of some of the challenges I faced after I became free, they were there. You taught me how to push through the pains so deep within that I tried to ignore them. But they would show up in my life as passive, childlike behaviors, and you would call me out. It is hard to hear the truth sometimes, but when someone cares about your well-being, you want them to share the things that you don't want to see in yourself. I recall a time when I was complaining about my current marriage. I was in school, working full-time, and had three part-time jobs. Wow! I experienced exhaustion writing that sentence.

I was complaining about how I shouldn't have to tell him to do certain things; he should know. For example, he knows I am going to the grocery store, so when I return home, even if he is watching a football game, he should hear the garage door open and know to help me with the groceries.

After I finished my rant, you calmly asked me, "Did you use your words?"

I looked at you and said, "What do you mean, did I use my words? It should be common sense. He should know."

You asked again, "Did you use your words?"

With some level of irritation in my voice, I said, "NO. I did not use my words."

You continued to say, "Well, he won't know until you open up your mouth and communicate your needs."

I did not want to hear that at all. Instead, I would slam the cabinets or make noise with everything I was putting away, hoping he would finally ask if I needed help. When he did, I had an attitude and nothing to say. I gave him the silent treatment, which is essentially passive-aggressive behavior. I finally listened to my sister, and guess what? Having a conversation worked, and even to this day, when I come home with groceries, who is coming out to assist me with them? Some of you may say that is a no-brainer. My man already does that. You must not have been doing something right. Well, let me say this: when you walk around with the demeanor that you don't need anybody and can do it all by yourself, as I did, then you will communicate through your actions that they are not required. Have you ever made someone feel like they were not needed in their own home?

Although you are not omnipresent, you have been with me during some of the most difficult times in my life. When my son was being abused by his ex-wife, you and my big brother allowed him to stay at your home on one of the occasions he attempted to leave the marriage. On average, it takes a person at least seven times to leave their abuser for good if they survive. You were with me and my son when we had to face the undesirable nature of simply being in family court. That was the first time the ex-wife stated (regarding me) that if I could not protect my children from a pedophile, how could I protect her children? I was in complete shock. I wanted to know what he shared with her. Then I feared one of my sons may have been sexually molested. As I sat in the courtroom, I could feel my eyes well up with tears; however, I did not want to give her the satisfaction of seeing my pain.

I had to leave the courtroom to compose myself, as I have dedicated my life to working with children, teens, and young adults, and have never been accused of such improprieties. I felt as though I was being abused all over again, but you were there. YOU were there to witness the idiotic behavior. The beauty of having someone like this in your life is that they don't just tell you what you want to hear to make things comfortable for you. YOU have always been honest with me, whether I was right or wrong, you would tell me. You always moved with love. You were this way with my sons as well. This is the type of human being that I pray everyone has in their life, because it is a demonstration of God's love. Even when He tells us to go left and we go right, in His loving way, He corrects us. He loves us so much that He ensures we have someone in our lives to remind us of His love.

I refer to my circle as my 'beauty of blooms.' I have an aunt who has shown up for me. She would agree that we have not always been close; however, as we both have matured and come into our womanhood, we have loved each other. She has been there to encourage and support me through some very tough times. When I reach out, whether by phone or text, she responds. What I love about her the most is that she sees good in every situation and reminds me that it will be alright, and to pray. Most importantly, we love each other, and if either one of us needed anything, we would be there, no questions asked. Some people think you have to talk to someone every day to be connected; however, you know you have something special when you can pick up where you left off as if no time has passed, and nobody has an attitude because you didn't call.

Throughout my life, I can think of women whom God has placed in my life. Some have only been with me for a season, and some are still with me. I could write a book on how each of them has impacted my life in various ways. I am even thankful for the women who were placed in my life who caused me harm. Their ways helped to strengthen my character and serve as the fertilizer that nourished my growth, enabling me to become the person I am today. It is true that what the enemy meant for evil, God will work out for His good. This certainly does not mean it was pleasant to experience pressure; however, the outcome was worth it.

Another bloom in my life was my maternal aunt, who passed away in October of 2013 after battling lung cancer. We would talk every Wednesday evening. She was very much aware of the strained relationship I had with her sister, and she stood in the gap. Not to assume the role of my mother, but to be what I needed in a mother during this difficult time. No matter how old you are, you always want the love of both of your parents, but here is the thing: you cannot make them do what they don't want to do. God gives each of us autonomy and free will. If He will not force you to choose Him, He certainly will not force a mother, father, aunt, uncle, or anyone to choose you. Well, my aunt understood her assignment and was what I needed her to be. In many ways, she welcomed the relationship and our closeness, having all boys. We talked every week about work, the weather, and whatever was on our minds. She would always end our calls in prayer. Now, my aunt was not always saved and would fight or tell someone about themselves in a heartbeat.

She was the one you always wanted to be on your side, no matter where you were going. When she accepted Christ, the energy didn't change, but her message did, and I am so grateful for all she was in my life. During one of our last conversations, she told me, "As hard as this may sound, you must live your life and stay prayed up. Your mother will never come to you while he (Mom's husband) is living. You have done everything you can do to mend the relationship. The only way you will be reunited with your mother is if he is no longer in her life. He has a hold on her that is too strong for you to break." This was difficult for me to hear, but I knew what she was saying was true.

For so long, I wondered what was wrong with me that I did not have the acceptance and love from my mother. I also have thought that not being able to see my grandkids was God's way of punishing me for my relationship with my mother. But I recall what my aunt said years before I became a grandmother; my mom's actions were based on a decision my mother made. It had nothing to do with me, and God would honor my efforts to mend things with her. Through her words, I realized I could do everything to resolve complicated situations with others in my life, but they must have the heart to receive. Only the Creator can fix things that He has created. I believe He has created me, and I trust that whatever is broken, only He can deem it necessary to fix.

I could go on and on about the imprints that have been placed on my heart of women who have been pivotal in my life. Through my experiences with those who have not had my best interest at heart and those who have, I've learned that God will always provide you with what you need and who you need. Despite your imperfections, flawed characteristics, and unhealed behaviors, the YOU who is in your life loves you through it. We often need YOU in our lives to remind us of God's love, His strength, and how He moves in us. It is YOU who reminds us of how big God is and what He can do when it feels like the world is caving in on us. It is YOU! No competition. No comparison. If I need anything, YOU are there to fulfill it. If YOU have a need, I am there to fulfill it. When you are sad, I will lift you. When YOU cry, I will wipe your tears. When I do not want to get out of bed, maybe you will lie in the bed with me for a little while; however, you will not allow me to stay there and wallow in my pain. You will remind me of what the Lord says, speak life into me, and walk through the pain with me. Through the laughs, through the tears, through the uncertainties, YOU have always been there, and WE will ALWAYS be there for each other. Be sure you have a YOU in your life, and the very thing they are or have been to you; make sure you are what they need you to be for them.

It is essential to have someone in our lives. It is also crucial for you to pour into others in the same way. How do you show up in the lives of others? Are you sisterly in that you would send your sister some money because you know she struggles with buying things for herself? Do you call and pray for your sister because you feel the pain in your soul that she needs you, so you send her encouraging words via text, mail, or a phone call? I was told once that we make time for what is important to us. It may not always be our intention to be so busy that we are only consumed with our needs; however, I have found that when we hold space for others, especially the women in our lives, the very thing we need or have been avoiding is with the YOU that YOU have in your life. It is this beautiful tapestry of love that God provides us. If you do not have one, please pray for God to send you one. You will be so glad you did.

REFLECTION QUESTIONS

1. Who is the beauty of bloom in your life? How have they shown up for you, and how have you shown up for them?

....

....

....

....

....

....

2. What do you value most in a friendship? In a sisterhood? What are some ways that you can encourage the YOU in your life? What do you need in a sister?

....

....

....

....

....

....

I AM BUILT DIFFERENT

"Being confident in this very thing, that he who hath begun a good work in you will perform it until the day of Jesus Christ." Philippians 1:6 (KJV)

Do you sometimes feel as though you are aimlessly walking through life, not really knowing what direction to take? Perhaps you have made some decisions in your life that have come at a price so high that you don't trust your ability to make a decision. So, you don't make one at all. Well, I have walked through life aimlessly, with some uncertainty, and questioning what I was supposed to do next. What is my purpose? Who am I? I know who I belong to in Christ, but clearly, I did not know who I am in Christ. I had lost sight of who God created me to be. He said that we are fearfully and wonderfully made. We are a peculiar people, a royal priesthood, but somehow, I have allowed people and situations to direct me outside of a path of who He says I am. God has equipped us with everything that we need. He has empowered us with abilities that demonstrate that those in Christ are built differently.

In Deuteronomy 28:13, the Lord says, He will make you the head, not the tail, if you pay attention to the commands of the Lord your God that He will give you this day and carefully follow them, you will always be at the top, never at the bottom.

You will be blessed in the city and blessed in the country. Wherever we go, we are blessed. Those who are connected to us will be blessed, as stated in Deuteronomy 28:4, and the fruit of our womb will also be blessed. He goes on to say that the enemies that revolt against us will be defeated before us. They will come at you from one direction and flee from you in seven. God's word is powerful. He is powerful. Our words are powerful. We are built differently. Remember, we are peculiar people. We were made in His image. If we could see ourselves the way He sees us, My God, the way we would walk into a room would be like knowing we are supposed to be there because He put us there.

There were so many distractions trying to prevent me from completing this book. Not only does the enemy want me to stay in bondage to my fear and my shame, but he also does not want anyone connected to me to win or to be free. What is it within us that is so powerful that the enemy does not want us to manifest it on this earth? I want to share with you something I recently encountered. I am absolutely, positively free if I can be this vulnerable with you to share this encounter. I call it an encounter because it's something I was not expecting. At the age of 12, I asked God for a specific spiritual gift, not understanding it would be more significant than something cool or something that would make me special. Some spiritual gifts were already operating within me. While communing with God, I was reading about the nine spiritual gifts. So, in my adolescent demeanor, I asked Him for all nine gifts. I expressed to Him how awesome that would be. As a pre-teen, when I asked God for something, I always believed He would give it to me. There is something about this type of faith. To be so attuned with God that you know that you know that you know. I allowed others to take me away from this type of faith, but God remained. He never left me.

One Wednesday night, I went to church service, and they were having an altar call. I went to the altar for prayer. Pastor A requested that I come forward. He whispered in my ear and said, "You have asked God for all nine gifts of the Holy Spirit. Now they will not all operate at the same time; however, if you want all nine gifts, God says you can have them. Are you ready to receive them?" There is no way that Pastor A could have known about my request to God unless God Himself revealed it. He prayed a dynamic prayer, and I received the nine gifts of the Spirit. The nine gifts of the Holy Spirit are the word of wisdom, the word of knowledge, faith, the gifts of healing, the working of miracles, prophecy, the discerning of spirits, different kinds of tongues, and the interpretation of tongues. This affirmed for me that God really does hear me when I pray. Perhaps there is something you have prayed for, and God has given it to you. The enemy does not want you to use it. He is doing what he can to distract you. To find a way for you not to fulfill what God has called you to do. He has nothing new, and we all know how his story ends. One thing I know about God is that He will give you the desires of your heart, and your requests will not return to you void. I believe that even in times of uncertainty, He will allow us to keep our gifts, and if we do not use them, He can certainly give them to someone who will.

As a teenager, I learned of the watch hours, times when Christians should pray because the devil is most active, and we are most unguarded. That does not mean, however, that the enemy is not moving throughout the day. However, when we are sleeping, we are most vulnerable to a demonic encounter. Typically, between 3:00 and 4:00 a.m. is the most active time for evil spirits. I have often had demonic encounters; however, they have been more frequent during the process of writing this book. On Wednesday, March 19th, approximately 4:30 am, I was preparing to travel to Dallas, Texas, for the "Women of Influence Luncheon" and a scheduled speaking engagement. The last time I had a demonic encounter was right before the book launch for *My Story. Your Hope,* (also in Dallas). You're probably asking, "What do you mean by a demonic encounter? "

Have you ever wrestled with the devil and known you were in a fight for your life? I typically do not sleep on my back because this leaves me the most vulnerable to physical and spiritual assault, so I have learned over the years to sleep on my side or on my stomach. That night before leaving for Dallas, I was sleeping on my stomach. My husband was preparing to leave for work and kissed me on my cheek as he typically does. Although I was lightly asleep, I could hear him reset the house alarm, walk out the door, and lock it. He did that twice, as always, to make sure the door was shut. I could hear the engine of his Ram dooly truck in the driveway warming up before he drove off. I am asleep, but not in a deep sleep, and minimally conscious. Then it happened. I could feel the weight of this spirit on my back.

Because I have had spiritual encounters throughout my life, I have come to understand the scripture, "We fight not against flesh and blood, but against principalities, against powers, against the rulers of the darkness of this age" (Ephesians 6:12, NKJV).

Knowing this, I still wanted to rationalize it away. I did not want it to be true. I would say it's sleep paralysis because that's a more acceptable explanation to share with others. It is more believable. However, I knew what I was experiencing was not a medical condition. It was spiritual, and the only way to overcome it was through the name above all names. I couldn't move. I awoke suddenly, recognizing what was happening. When this happened previously, I would be so paralyzed with fear that I kept my eyes closed. I dared to share those previous experiences with someone years ago, and the spiritual guidance they shared was pivotal: "Call out the name of Jesus. Hearing that name, the demon will flee." However, the enemy made my mouth feel muzzled. I could not open my mouth. This is always the case when I have an encounter. Even Satan knows there is power in the name of Jesus. I tried to raise myself and open my mouth. I was trying with all my might to get out, "Jesus." An inexplicable, suffocating force felt like it was upon me. I was helpless. Previously, when I couldn't verbally say Jesus' name, I would speak it in my mind.

There I was, looking fear in the eye. As I am trying to lift my head, the force of the demon pressed me down. I was angry! I muttered, "You are bold. You literally showed up immediately after my husband left the home. You showed up to challenge my faith and my belief in myself and the word. You are challenging whether I can let go of fear." I was finally able to lift my head. Not because the demon gave in, but because it was by God's Spirit. I lifted my head and turned towards the demon, my eyes open. I heard a forceful wind as I looked it in the eyes and uttered softly at first, "Jesus." For the first time in my life, I felt the power of the name of Jesus. The strength of His name demanded that the demon flee. The sound of the rushing wind that I could hear, the enormous strength that I could feel, demanded that this spirit leave quickly. Can you imagine someone having so much power that when you muddle their name, they MUST respond?! I began to weep, from weeping I began to repent, questioning whether I had done something to allow this evil presence to enter my home, to praising God.

From praising God, I began to worship God. Amongst all of this, the Lord had me send an email to a student in response to something I had inquired about. I did not understand why I needed to send it at 5:11 am; however, I did. During Lent, I had given up fear and negativity. That encounter was a test to see if I was free from the stronghold of fear. When there is something in you that the devil does not want to manifest, he will do everything he can to prevent it. No one can ever tell me that there is no God. I have experienced the power of His name. Every knee shall bow, and every tongue will confess that He is Lord. As the day went on, I felt drained. It was like that feeling when the Holy Spirit is working in you, and you have praised God for all His good works. This felt more like heaviness. Something that I could not shake. I had been in a fight.

I have learned the hard way that obedience is better than sacrifice, and so when God tells me to do something, I do it. I may try to negotiate a little, but I do what He tells me to do. Remember, I told you I emailed a student early one morning? Well, during class, the Holy Spirit instructed me to send her a direct message in the Zoom chat, so I did. I requested to speak with her after class regarding a spiritual question. I know it sounds very unorthodox. Why this student? Well, at the beginning of the course, I had students introduce themselves, and one of them shared that she is a minister. She exuded peace and positivity. She made you feel safe knowing her. A feeling that, as a clinician, you want others to feel in your space. During our discussion, she shared that she had been having a difficult time in class because she wanted to share something with me. She was having some reservations about doing so and continued to pray throughout class. When I sent her the message, she felt released to share.

After class, she told me that when she first received my message, she thought, "Why is Dr. C up so early?" She then said the Holy Spirit instructed her to pray for me and my son. You may not know who is praying for you, but please know that God has assigned someone specifically to keep you covered. She began to tell me that "things have been happening around you, but they will not happen to you." She was right. I had been witnessing hurt and harm to others. I witnessed a driver crash into a tree. It was devastating to watch. I later learned of his death. I was hearing or seeing something adversely impact others, and it saddened me. She went on to say that the demon I fought with was sent to get my attention. She shared, "God needed you to know and feel His power. You were able to open your eyes because you are strong enough now to fight the demons that have been attacking you. You did not have the strength in the past. The level that God is preparing you for will require you to fight greater demons. You have passed a huge test of obedience; nothing can stop you now." She went on to say, "The devil is after a son; he is after his mind, you must keep him covered, and you must keep anointed oil with you at all times. Be mindful of your eye gate. He is trying to cut off your voice. He does not want this book to be released into the world. He is making you a witness to His power. You now have Godfidence." The Holy Spirit was using her as a vessel, and it was flowing so quickly that at times I was overwhelmed with tears, and I couldn't write it down fast enough. I could literally feel His presence radiate from the computer screen.

I wasn't sure which son she was referring to, but I texted my oldest son, telling him I needed to talk to him and share something with him. When I told him about what the Holy Spirit said, he became quiet. He asked, "How do you know it's me?" I told him I didn't know for sure; I was being obedient in sharing it with him. He paused for a moment and said, "Each day is a battle. Each day, I must fight to get up because I am constantly reminded of the separation from my sons. Sometimes it is hard to keep going, but I keep pushing, I keep loving, I keep helping others in hopes that God will help me." I shared with him that the Lord has moved him to do something, but he has not taken action. The movement was subtle, but it was a move, nonetheless. This encounter and this prophecy have truly impacted my life and my relationship with God. What the enemy meant as continued fear and destruction, God has turned it around for His good. There is not a space that I have entered since this encounter that I feel small, because I know who is with me. There is no space I have entered where I feel inferior. Now, don't get it twisted, the enemy is still taking his best shots through the whispers in my head. However, it hits a little differently now. It has not penetrated my heart or my mind because of the transformative power of God. I pray more now than I did before. I am more intentional in what I say and how I treat others. I do not have time to play about anything that is attached to me. God has emboldened me to do what He has purposed in my heart to do. I encourage you to put on the whole armor of God, look your demons in the eye, and say the name of Jesus! If I did not believe in His power, His dominion on this earth, I do now! There is nothing impossible with God. There is nothing that I do not think He can do.

You may be struggling to define who you are and what your purpose in life is. I know I have. It has taken me some time to realize that carving out my own path with God's guidance is the right thing to do.

Do you ever try to take on characteristics of others, because if you do, you are robbing yourself? To exist in a state of comparison implies you lack fulfillment. I purchased what I thought was a Louis Vuitton handbag. I was so excited. From a distance, it looked like all the others. When the handle began to break down in the strands, the leather started to become fragmented, the inner lining began to tear, and the authenticity of the bag became a concern. Its appearance no longer looked like the others. Its inauthenticity was revealed. I was told I could take it to a Louis Vuitton store, and they would restore it to their high standards of craftsmanship. The truth is, I wasn't sure who manufactured this bag, but it did not have the Louis Vuitton DNA. Authentic LVs have a stamp on the inside with a number, placed by the designer, which authenticates their product. Newer handbags by LV have a microchip that can be scanned at their store. To authenticate means to prove that something is real, genuine, or valid. When you do not embrace who you truly are, you exist as a counterfeit. You are not at all who God has designed you to be. No matter how much you try to be someone other than yourself, you cannot duplicate authenticity when it comes from God. When God created you, He designed you in

His image. There is no one like you. You are fearfully and wonderfully made. I hope that you will begin to see yourself as God sees you and walk into every room with purpose, like you know Who sent you.

There was a point in my life when I would ask why I had to be the product of brokenness. To be the child of parents who had not addressed their own needs and had figured out their identity before bringing me into the world. Why did I choose from my place of pain and select a partner as a father, who was also broken, a narcissist, and an abuser? Why did I continue the generational trauma that nearly consumed us? I stopped asking why and began to appreciate each lesson taught and what it revealed. Whether the trial was sent by God or by the enemy, God kept me and everything attached to me throughout the process.

REFLECTION QUESTIONS:

1. How have the challenges in your life strengthened you? What has God brought you through that He wants you to share to help someone else?

2. What concerns do you have about sharing your story?

3. How can you begin to share the goodness of God to help others?

PEACE WITHIN

"Peace, I leave with you; my peace I give you. I do not give to you as the world gives. Do not let your hearts be troubled and do not be afraid. "John 14:28 NIV

When I decided a few years back to create a Facebook profile page, I wondered about what type of profile image I would share. I was sure it would not be a picture of me, because at the time, I was not ready to be visible for others to examine or potentially criticize. I chose a picture from an event hosted by a high school organization I helped sponsor. The event was held at a well-visited science museum. The image was created on a large, interactive game with bright, light elements, and I pegged the photo "I love you!" Instead of the word "love," I created a heart and an upward arrow for "you." This was representative of how I feel about others.

In addition to including an image, you could also include typed words. Under the image, I typed the words "strength within." These two words described how I viewed myself as one who had conquered what should have killed me. It spoke to all the pain I had endured as a child and what I had overcome from my tumultuous marriage. I believed I had done incredible work to be in a place of survival. I had overcome. I am strong. I am that woman! God truly had brought me through the fire without the appearance of what I had literally gone through. Believing that my current situation could not have occurred without God, I still felt something was missing. I still felt this need to fix whatever I saw as being broken. I would let things and situations go, then pick them back up again. The exhaustion of always trying to make space for others and fix things that I had not broken consumed me. I realized strength is great, but peace is true strength. When you can let go and place every care in the world in God's hands, a calmness resides within, and you believe to live, not moved by what is occurring around you. Although I cannot see the air that I breathe, I know it is there. I do not question where the air is coming from. It is similar to my peace in Christ. I do not question whether He will provide it. Or whether He is going to heal or anything else. I stand on His promises and have experienced that peace that surpasses my understanding. It is a peace He gives that provides me with great confidence that reconciles, unites, and transforms. When peace comes from within, there is no external struggle or uncertainty that can diminish.

This does not mean life will not challenge us; however, when we make Jesus our center and focus on Him, rather than our circumstances, we allow His peace to rule in our lives and in our hearts. When you embrace this meaning, you truly will experience peace within. Many of my lived experiences remind me of the promise that God made to the three Hebrew boys who were in the fiery furnace. Those three boys had a level of peace and assurance that only God could give. They had an unshakeable faith and confidence in God, even in the face of death. Having confidence in God means trusting Him in the fire, in situations that are uncomfortable and sometimes fearful. Not just outside of the fire. Whether He delivers or not, He is still God, and He is still good. Every situation I have ever gone through has given me strength and a firm belief in Him. I stand today because I was not consumed by the fire but empowered by it.

SOURCES CITED

American Psychiatric Association. (2013). Diagnostic and
statistical manual of mental disorders (5th ed.). Washington,
DC: Author.

Centers for Disease Control and Prevention. (2024, May 16).
About intimate partner violence. https://www.cdc.gov/
intimate-partner-violence/about/index.html

Oxford University Press. (n.d.). Mask. In Oxford English
Dictionary. Retrieved August 15, 2025, from https://www.
oed.com/search/dictionary/?scope=Entries&q=mask